# The Psalter for Christian Worship

# The Psalter for Christian Worship

## Michael Morgan

Witherspoon Press
Louisville, Kentucky

Office of Theology
and Worship
Louisville, Kentucky

COLUMBIA
THEOLOGICAL
SEMINARY

Columbia Theological
Seminary
Decatur, Georgia

*Edited by Paul Detterman*

*Book interior and cover design by Claire Calhoun*

*First edition*

Published by Witherspoon Press, a Ministry of the General Assembly
Council, Congregational Ministries Division, Presbyterian Church (U.S.A.),
Louisville, Kentucky, in partnership with the Office of Theology and
Worship and Columbia Theological Seminary.

Web site address: http://www.pcusa.org/pcusa/witherspoon

PRINTED IN THE UNITED STATES OF AMERICA

99 00 01 02 03 04 05 06 07 08 — 10 9 8 7 6 5 4 3 2 1


The Library of Congress has cataloged the hardcover edition as follows:

**Library of Congress Cataloging-in-Publication Data**

Morgan, Michael, date.
      The Psalter for Christian worship / Michael Morgan. — 1st ed.
      p.    cm.
   ISBN 1-57153-013-4
   ISBN 1-57153-026-6 (pbk)
      1. Reformed Church—Liturgy—Texts. 2. Psalters—Texts.
I. Title.
BX9427.5.P74M67 1999
264'. 05137015—dc21

                                                           98-31861

*To the congregation of*
*Central Presbyterian Church, Atlanta;*
*my colleagues Ted, Kim, Marilyn, and Paul;*
*Richard;*
*and to all who would find on these pages*
*the words to frame their*
*prayers and praise.*

*This book is dedicated*
*with much devotion and love.*

# Contents

Preface . . . . . . . . . . . xi

Introduction . . . . . . . 1

## The Psalms

### Book I

Psalm 1 . . . . . . . . . . . 11
Psalm 2 . . . . . . . . . . . 12
Psalm 3 . . . . . . . . . . . 13
Psalm 4 . . . . . . . . . . . 14
Psalm 5 . . . . . . . . . . . 15
Psalm 6 . . . . . . . . . . . 16
Psalm 7 . . . . . . . . . . . 17
Psalm 8 . . . . . . . . . . . 18
Psalm 9 . . . . . . . . . . . 19
Psalm 10 . . . . . . . . . . 20
Psalm 11 . . . . . . . . . . 21
Psalm 12 . . . . . . . . . . 22
Psalm 13 . . . . . . . . . . 23
Psalm 14 . . . . . . . . . . 24
Psalm 15 . . . . . . . . . . 25
Psalm 16 . . . . . . . . . . 26
Psalm 17 . . . . . . . . . . 27
Psalm 18 . . . . . . . . . . 28
Psalm 19 . . . . . . . . . . 29
Psalm 20 . . . . . . . . . . 30
Psalm 21 . . . . . . . . . . 31
Psalm 22a . . . . . . . . . . 32

Psalm 22b . . . . . . . . . 33
Psalm 23 . . . . . . . . . . 34
Psalm 24 . . . . . . . . . . 35
Psalm 25 . . . . . . . . . . 36
Psalm 26 . . . . . . . . . . 37
Psalm 27 . . . . . . . . . . 38
Psalm 28 . . . . . . . . . . 39
Psalm 29 . . . . . . . . . . 40
Psalm 30 . . . . . . . . . . 41
Psalm 31a . . . . . . . . . 42
Psalm 31b . . . . . . . . . 43
Psalm 32 . . . . . . . . . . 44
Psalm 33 . . . . . . . . . . 45
Psalm 34 . . . . . . . . . . 46
Psalm 35 . . . . . . . . . . 47
Psalm 36 . . . . . . . . . . 48
Psalm 37 . . . . . . . . . . 49
Psalm 38 . . . . . . . . . . 50
Psalm 39 . . . . . . . . . . 51
Psalm 40 . . . . . . . . . . 52
Psalm 41 . . . . . . . . . . 53

### Book II

Psalm 42 . . . . . . . . . . 54
Psalm 43 . . . . . . . . . . 55
Psalm 44 . . . . . . . . . . 56
Psalm 45a . . . . . . . . . 57
Psalm 45b . . . . . . . . . 58
Psalm 46 . . . . . . . . . . 59

Psalm 47 . . . . . . . . . . 60
Psalm 48 . . . . . . . . . . 61
Psalm 49 . . . . . . . . . . 62
Psalm 50 . . . . . . . . . . 63
Psalm 51 . . . . . . . . . . 64
Psalm 52 . . . . . . . . . . 65
Psalm 53 . . . . . . . . . . 66
Psalm 54 . . . . . . . . . . 67
Psalm 55 . . . . . . . . . . 68
Psalm 56 . . . . . . . . . . 69
Psalm 57 . . . . . . . . . . 70
Psalm 58 . . . . . . . . . . 71
Psalm 59 . . . . . . . . . . 72
Psalm 60 . . . . . . . . . . 73
Psalm 61 . . . . . . . . . . 74
Psalm 62 . . . . . . . . . . 75
Psalm 63 . . . . . . . . . . 76
Psalm 64 . . . . . . . . . . 77
Psalm 65 . . . . . . . . . . 78
Psalm 66a . . . . . . . . . . 79
Psalm 66b . . . . . . . . . . 80
Psalm 67 . . . . . . . . . . 81
Psalm 68 . . . . . . . . . . 82
Psalm 69 . . . . . . . . . . 83
Psalm 70 . . . . . . . . . . 84
Psalm 71 . . . . . . . . . . 85
Psalm 72 . . . . . . . . . . 86

## Book III

Psalm 73 . . . . . . . . . . 87
Psalm 74 . . . . . . . . . . 88
Psalm 75 . . . . . . . . . . 89

Psalm 76 . . . . . . . . . . 90
Psalm 77 . . . . . . . . . . 91
Psalm 78 . . . . . . . . . . 92
Psalm 79 . . . . . . . . . . 93
Psalm 80 . . . . . . . . . . 94
Psalm 81 . . . . . . . . . . 95
Psalm 82 . . . . . . . . . . 96
Psalm 83 . . . . . . . . . . 97
Psalm 84 . . . . . . . . . . 98
Psalm 85 . . . . . . . . . . 99
Psalm 86 . . . . . . . . . . 100
Psalm 87 . . . . . . . . . . 101
Psalm 88 . . . . . . . . . . 102
Psalm 89a . . . . . . . . . . 103
Psalm 89b . . . . . . . . . . 104

## Book IV

Psalm 90 . . . . . . . . . . 105
Psalm 91 . . . . . . . . . . 106
Psalm 92 . . . . . . . . . . 107
Psalm 93 . . . . . . . . . . 108
Psalm 94 . . . . . . . . . . 109
Psalm 95 . . . . . . . . . . 110
Psalm 96 . . . . . . . . . . 111
Psalm 97 . . . . . . . . . . 112
Psalm 98 . . . . . . . . . . 113
Psalm 99 . . . . . . . . . . 114
Psalm 100 . . . . . . . . . . 115
Psalm 101 . . . . . . . . . . 116
Psalm 102 . . . . . . . . . . 117
Psalm 103 . . . . . . . . . . 118
Psalm 104a . . . . . . . . . . 119

| | |
|---|---|
| Psalm 104b ........ 120 | Psalm 129 ........ 150 |
| Psalm 105a ........ 121 | Psalm 130 ........ 151 |
| Psalm 105b ........ 122 | Psalm 131 ........ 152 |
| Psalm 106 ........ 123 | Psalm 132 ........ 153 |
| | Psalm 133 ........ 154 |

**Book V**

| | |
|---|---|
| | Psalm 134 ........ 155 |
| Psalm 107 ........ 124 | Psalm 135 ........ 156 |
| Psalm 108 ........ 125 | Psalm 136 ........ 157 |
| Psalm 109 ........ 126 | Psalm 137 ........ 158 |
| Psalm 110 ........ 127 | Psalm 138 ........ 159 |
| Psalm 111 ........ 128 | Psalm 139 ........ 160 |
| Psalm 112 ........ 129 | Psalm 140 ........ 161 |
| Psalm 113 ........ 130 | Psalm 141 ........ 162 |
| Psalm 114 ........ 131 | Psalm 142 ........ 163 |
| Psalm 115 ........ 132 | Psalm 143 ........ 164 |
| Psalm 116 ........ 133 | Psalm 144 ........ 165 |
| Psalm 117 ........ 134 | Psalm 145 ........ 166 |
| Psalm 118 ........ 135 | Psalm 146 ........ 167 |
| Psalm 119a ........ 136 | Psalm 147a ........ 168 |
| Psalm 119b ........ 137 | Psalm 147b ........ 169 |
| Psalm 119c ........ 138 | Psalm 148 ........ 170 |
| Psalm 119d ........ 139 | Psalm 149 ........ 171 |
| Psalm 119e ........ 140 | Psalm 150 ........ 172 |
| Psalm 120 ........ 141 | |
| Psalm 121 ........ 142 | Index of Suggested |
| Psalm 122 ........ 143 | Tunes ........ 173 |
| Psalm 123 ........ 144 | |
| Psalm 124 ........ 145 | Index of Liturgical |
| Psalm 125 ........ 146 | Use ........ 179 |
| Psalm 126 ........ 147 | |
| Psalm 127 ........ 148 | |
| Psalm 128 ........ 149 | |

# Preface

It was in the spirit of restoring metrical psalm singing to
the worship of our particular congregation, Central
Presbyterian Church in Atlanta, Georgia, that The
Reverend Dr. Theodore Wardlaw, pastor, invited me to
search through my collection of early psalters for
interesting paraphrases of lectionary psalms that we
could sing for the seven Sundays of the season of Easter.
I immediately examined Sternhold and Hopkins, Tate
and Brady, the Scottish Psalters of 1564 and 1650,
Archbishop Parker, Ainsworth, and perhaps fifty other
metrical versions and had to report that we could not
sing any of them, except as historical novelties, without
considerable revision.

As Isaac Watts's father advised him nearly three
centuries ago, "If you don't like the old psalms, write
some new ones," Ted challenged me to do the same. My
first attempts at versifying the psalms were so well
received by the congregation that I was urged to look
ahead to the Advent cycle. The next few weeks found me
immersed in my work, and by the end of the summer I
was able to present Central Church with a complete
version of the psalms in meter, which we continue to sing
every Sunday as the Lectionary dictates, to tunes our
congregation knows by heart.

I do not presume to be a scholar of linguistics. Rather,
I put my trust in those who over the centuries have given
us translations and paraphrases. Ever before me were the
Authorized Version (King James), the Prayer Book
Psalter, the New Revised Standard Version of the Bible,
and any of a dozen or so independent versions of the
psalms. My approach to each text was the same: to
condense thought and repetition into single units,
paraphrasing those to achieve the sense of the psalm.
When my own understanding was shallow, I sought help
in commentaries and devotionals from Calvin and Horne,

to Dahood and Brueggemann. Where the *Revised Common Lectionary* abbreviated the texts or divided the longer psalms, I considered the same alignment in my own version.

Never before have I embarked on such a meaningful and self-illuminating devotional exercise. I repeatedly found my own life experience reflected in the psalms on which I worked. Often, I would struggle with a particular psalm with no insight or inspiration at all, and in frustration turn to another, where the words would flow almost as quickly as I could write. Sometimes the first line to come to me would be halfway down the page, and the text would grow from there in both directions until the psalm was complete.

If certain texts read like those of a seventeenth-century divine, it is because I am so thoroughly steeped in the grandeur of their linguistic style. My frequent use of "Thee" and "Thou" for the Deity, along with the expected verb forms, reflects a passion for tradition and the belief that the language of our worship and our interaction with God transcends our daily conversation with each other. I have also been sensitive to inclusive language, both in reference to God and to the children of God.

I have not "Christianized" the psalms to the point of compromising their Old Testament character, but have tried to balance, wherever they are present, judgment with justice and vengeance with grace. Throughout this project, I have set my goal to be as true as possible to the Hebrew psalmist and the New Testament Messiah, to the shepherd boy and the Good Shepherd, ever striving to be poetic and not pedestrian in my quest to render the psalms as a meaningful expression of our faith.

Special appreciation is given to the following individuals who were kind enough to read the manuscript with a critical eye and ear for poetry and theology: Hal Hopson, Richard Peek, and Hubert and Claire Taylor (my predecessors at Central Church);

Christina Sizemore, a choir member at Central and an English professor; Harrison Taylor, my colleague from the old Council on Theology and Culture days; Dyana Haik, who traveled over a thousand miles to attend my first "Psalm-fest"; Paul Detterman, Associate for Worship in the Office of Theology and Worship, PC(USA); and Dr. Walter Brueggemann and Porter Remington of Columbia Theological Seminary. I am very grateful to Richard Ezell, who was unfailing in his patience to read text, sing tunes, make suggestions, and endure my devotion to this work. Without the encouragement of my congregation at Central Presbyterian Church, and the generous support of Columbia Theological Seminary through the efforts of its president, Dr. Douglas Oldenburg, this version of the psalms could never have become a reality.

# INTRODUCTION

## The Psalms, Worship, and the Reformed Tradition

Metrical psalmody: Even the name can sound intimidating and as austere as anything one might associate with staid Scottish Presbyterians! Yet little else is closer to the heart of worship in the Reformed tradition than the Psalms of David paraphrased in metered verse. Over four hundred years ago, our first service book, the *Forme of Prayers and Ministration of the Sacraments,* was beloved by the people for the metrical psalter it contained.

The singing of psalms has always been an integral part of Christian worship. Prior to the Reformation, however, liturgical music had gradually become more the possession of the church and less a treasure of the people. In their Latin version, which few could understand, psalms in worship were sung to plainchant melodies. Gregorian chant may be a pure and expressive means of conveying the prose of the Latin Bible, but it is far less effective with poetry. The use of chant also required most of the service music to be "performed" by trained singers who could read musical notation, while the congregation sang only the simplest responses. As more intricate service music evolved, even these responses became the property of the choir, leaving the people to passively observe the liturgy.

If liturgical music was to be returned to the people, three things had to be accomplished:

1. Texts had to return to the vernacular in order to be meaningful to those who sang them. The beauty of Latin never made it past the ears of many listeners. It

was the language they used with each other that Christians desired for their communication with God and to hear God speaking to them.

2. Texts had to be cast in a form that people could read, memorize, and assimilate with ease. Short phrases, structured within a variety of rhyme schemes, made texts more comprehensible.

3. A type of music had to be devised that untrained voices could sing. The rich complexities crafted by Giovanni Palestrina (d. 1594), William Byrd (1534–1623), and Thomas Tallis (1505–1585) may have enveloped worshipers in a reverberant swirl of sound, but the simple ballads they knew by heart sustained them through the remainder of the week.

## John Calvin's Psalter

For Christians who embraced the sixteenth-century Genevan reforms, John Calvin's innovative psalmody was a fitting solution. Calvin (1509–1564) felt that only those songs which were given to us by God, the biblical psalms, were worthy of our giving back to God. With few exceptions, he desired that only the Psalms of David be sung in worship.

It was essential that psalms be in the vernacular, and Calvin, knowing this required translation anyway, allowed the texts to be rendered in verse. He engaged the poet Clement Marot (c. 1497-1544) and the theologian Theodore de Bèze (1519–1605) to accomplish his goal: to transform ancient Hebrew verse into the finest French poetry of the day.

## English Psalters

The English metrical psalter and the first Scottish psalter found more humble genesis in the psalm "ballads" composed by Thomas Sternhold (1500–1549), a groom in the chamber of King Henry VIII. Sternhold was no poetic match for Marot, but English-speaking Christians had never before sung psalms in their own language, and young Edward, the future king, upon hearing Sternhold singing one of his verses, encouraged him to write more.

Within a few years, both servant and king were dead, and under the violent reign of Mary Tudor, the Church in England renounced many elements of the Reformation. Protestants fled to the Continent where Reformers were finding acceptance, if not always welcome. Inspired and informed by the teachings of Calvin, these English Protestants set out to complete a Psalter, incorporating the work of Sternhold, but also drawing on the talents of John Hopkins (d. 1570), William Whittingham (1520–1579), William Kethe (d. 1608), and others. The completed "Sternhold and Hopkins" version, popularly known as the "Old Version," was published in 1562. Scottish refugees, under the leadership of John Knox (1505–1572), were not satisfied with an identical psalter to the English, and in 1564 they published their own version, in which about a third of the texts differed from Sternhold and Hopkins.

Music found in both psalters came primarily from the same sources: popular adaptations of some of the new hymns of the Reformation, and original tunes contributed primarily by Louis Bourgeois (1510–1561). As a reaction to the complex music of the pre-Reformation Church, the music, prescribed by Calvin, was in unison so that the congregation might lift a common voice to God without the "clutter" of harmony, counterpoint, or instrumental accompaniment. The wonderful tunes of Bourgeois brought melodic and rhythmic freshness to singing.

Protestants who returned to England during the reign of Queen Elizabeth I brought their psalter home with them. With occasional revision, this translation was retained for the next two hundred years. Competitive metrical versions appeared, most notably the 1612 psalter by Henry Ainsworth (1571–1622) and the 1632 collection by George Wither (1588–1667), but these appealed to the fringes of the Anglican communion rather than its core. Even the "New Version" of Nahum Tate (1652–1715) and Nicholas Brady (1659–1726), published in 1696 to replace the archaic "Old Version," met with little enthusiasm. The much-loved verses of Sternhold and Hopkins continued to be sung into the nineteenth century.

## Scottish Psalters

Throughout this time, the Scottish were in conflict with the English over a variety of matters both political and religious. Their own Queen Mary was put to death by Elizabeth I, who later died with no apparent heir. Elizabeth was succeeded by James I, the son of her Scottish adversary. With the ascent of King James (1603), the Tudor succession ended and the Stuart line began. The two countries were united. The national churches, however, had become too distinct to merge and too entrenched to compromise. From the form of church government and ordering of worship to the form of the psalms they sang, one sought independence and the other sought control.

The final assault by the English Church, led by Archbishop Laud, was to force the Anglican Book of Common Prayer on the Church of Scotland. Appended to this liturgy was a new psalter, attributed to the late King James himself, which Laud believed would make the new service more palatable to the Scots. The plan failed miserably, and triggered a civil war with England, which ended with the execution of Charles I and the institution of the Commonwealth under Oliver Cromwell.

With the new power they were enjoying at the expense of the English, the Scots and the Puritans abrogated the use of the Anglican prayer book in favor of their own Directory for Worship, and sought to replace the 1564 Scottish Psalter with one that was uniquely their own. The Westminster Assembly (1643–1653) examined versions by William Barton (1603–1678), Francis Rous (1579–1659), and others, and in 1650 published their psalter, "more plaine, smooth and agreeable to the Text, than any heretofore." The publication of this version, known simply as the "Scottish Psalter," delineated English and Scottish psalmody, setting a metrical standard for the Church of Scotland and other English-speaking Presbyterians, which remains virtually unchallenged to this day.

## Eighteenth and Nineteenth Centuries

From the beginning of the Reformation, the texts of the Hebrew psalms have presented a perpetual dilemma for Christians. Many verses in the psalms applied so directly to the experience of the Hebrew people in their struggle or spoke so intimately of the anger and frustration of the psalmist that they were thought suitable to be sung by Christians. Further, early metrical settings adhered so strictly to the original Hebrew that twenty or thirty stanzas were required at times to communicate the full psalm text. Restricted to the use of the psalms alone in worship, there was no proclamation of the Gospel through congregational song. Surely praise, thanksgiving, mercy, grace, and redemption were present in the psalms, but the realization of God's covenant through the gift of Jesus Christ was nowhere to be found. The efforts of John Patrick (1632–1695), Isaac Watts (1674–1748), and others brought the psalter into conversation with the New Testament through more liberal paraphrase.

A second problem remains a current challenge: the difficulty of producing a metrical version of the psalms that can be called "poetry," when these texts are to be sung by a congregation at worship. Some of the more "poetic" paraphrases of the psalms, such as those of

James Merrick (1720–1769) seem too "sublime" to be confined to the monotony of a long-meter or common-meter tune. This may be one more reason why many great poets, George Herbert (1593–1632), John Donne (1572–1631), and John Milton (1608–1674) among them, did not attempt to turn the whole psalter into verse, choosing instead to select only those psalms that most appealed to them.

The reading of the Hebrew text through New Testament eyes, especially in those versions which "Christianized" the psalms, and the loosening of the reins that psalmody held on church music to allow paraphrases of other portions of Scripture, kept portions of the psalter, in the repertoire of many congregations. However, the "culprit" in the near demise of metrical psalmody was not the psalms themselves, but performance practice. Since many people could not read music, they depended on a leader, or "precentor" to "line out" the psalms. The tune would be sung, line by line, with the congregation responding, line by line, in echo fashion. So as not to tax the communicants' tonal memories, the psalms were often sung at a snail's pace, with little of the energy Bourgeois had written into his original tunes.

To simplify singing even more, only a dozen tunes were allowed for many years, with the hope that congregations would eventually learn them. There are amusing stories of psalm singing in worship where the people sang their favorite tune without regard for the precentor or the rest of the congregation, resulting in what was described by one contemporary critic as a sound that resembled the bleating of sheep on the moors! It soon became the fashion for precentors to ornament and embellish the psalm tune with "graces," which so disguised the melodies that congregations were challenged to identify, much less reproduce them.

In an attempt to salvage metrical psalmody, some presbyteries restricted the singing in worship to choirs comprised of parishioners who were willing to learn to sing. Precentors became music educators and offered instruction in singing psalm tunes. The psalm texts were considered by some to be too sacrosanct to be sung outside of worship, so "practice verses" were written to be substituted for the psalm when learning the music and then discarded at the church door. These texts were personal, secular, and even earthy at times, but singing meant so much to the people that they endured the instruction in order to sing in the choir, and soon some of the choir lofts held more people than the naves.

By the Victorian era and the early twentieth century, psalmody had for the most part been swallowed up in a vast sea of hymns authored by the Wesleys, the poets of the Oxford movement, and many other independent hymn writers.

## Contemporary Psalters

As metrical psalms disappeared from regular use in worship, prose settings of the psalms, which had endured in other liturgical traditions, began to take their place. Lectionaries, whether strictly observed or not, regularly included psalms among the lessons. Since there existed no less imaginative way for a congregation to raise a psalm than as a responsive reading, those charged with fostering creative and meaningful corporate worship began to seek ways to improve prose psalmody. The ancient practice of antiphonal singing, with repeated phrases sung in response to portions of a psalm, became a popular "innovation" in churches for whom that tradition had long been lost. Congregations could easily learn the refrain and sing "on cue" while the choir chanted the psalm verses. These responses or "antiphons" gave the people a means of participating in the singing of the psalms, though not with the complete involvement that metrical psalmody afforded.

The Christian church, at the end of the millennium, is

experiencing a time of liturgical renewal, with increased interest in reclaiming traditions and elements of Reformed faith and practice. One of those traditions is metrical psalmody, as evidenced in the proliferation of psalm settings in many current denominational hymnals within the Reformed tradition. *Rejoice in the Lord* (1985), the *Psalter Hymnal* (1987), and *The Presbyterian Hymnal* (1990) each contain psalm settings in a variety of styles: meter, prose, blank verse, rhyme, chant, and antiphon. None are as accessible to a wide range of worshipers as a metrical psalm sung to a familiar tune.

Michael Morgan
Paul Detterman

# THE PSALMS

# Book I

## Psalm 1

*A Wisdom Psalm*

How blest are they who venture not
    Into the dark and sinful way,
But find delight in God's own law,
    And contemplate it night and day.

As trees beside the stream they grow
    And flourish, wholesome fruit they bear;
The wicked lot are cast aside
    And lost to their own dark despair.

The judgment of the LORD is sure
    And good to those who seek God's face;
The righteous find themselves redeemed,
    And heirs to God's all-knowing grace.

# Psalm 2

*A Royal Psalm*

Why do nations rage together;
    Why in vain do they conspire?
Rulers of earth's vast dominions
    Light the skies with martyrs' fire.
Truth mistaken, God forsaken,
    Banes of righteousness arise;
Yet shall they reap sore displeasure,
    Sure defeat before God's eyes.

To the children of the promise
    God shall give the throne this day;
With a scepter forged of iron,
    They shall dash their foes as clay.
Faith revealing, humbly kneeling,
    Quench the fire and sheathe the sword;
For God's wrath is quickly kindled;
    Blest are they who serve the LORD.

# Psalm 3

*A Lament*

O LORD, how many are my foes!
    How vast their legions seem to be!
From ev'ry side, their threats deride,
    And work to shake my faith in Thee.

But Thou, O LORD, remain my shield,
    My glory and Redeemer still;
I cry to Thee, who answers me,
    Steadfastly from Thy holy hill.

My eyes are closed, I sleep in peace,
    Assured that I again will wake;
When arms shall raise, I'll give Thee praise,
    Rejoicing for Thy mercy's sake.

Arise, O LORD, deliver me
    From all who would my life assail;
Thy blessing sure will long endure,
    And righteousness at last prevail.

# Psalm 4

*A Lament*


God of all righteousness, hear when I pray,
  In my distress be my hope and my stay;
Long I have suffered revilement and shame,
  Great God of mercy, I call on Your name.

Angry, yet silent, I know there will be
  Justice according to holy decree;
Never to answer corruption in kind,
  But in Your promise true peace will I find.

When those around me my faith would confound,
  May I rejoice in Your gifts that abound;
Peace and assurance all discord withstand,
  Safely I rest in the palm of Your hand.

# Psalm 5

*A Morning Prayer*

O hear the words I speak, my God,
    To my unuttered sighs attend;
And from Thine overwhelming throne
    To my frail spirit, grace extend.

For early shall my prayers ascend
    Like incense rising to the sky;
In confidence, I make my plea,
    And in Thy faithfulness rely.

Thy heart delights in all things good,
    And evil flees if Thou art there;
Thy truth will over pride prevail,
    And justice shall be brought to bear.

But through the bounty of Thy love
    Among Thy chosen I am cast,
O lead me forth in righteousness,
    And bring me safely home at last.

# Psalm 6

*A Prayer for Mercy*

LORD, rebuke me not in wrath,
    Nor in anger hide Your face;
Vast the heights of agony,
    Great the depths of my disgrace.
Flesh and spirit languish sore,
O forget my soul no more.

LORD, Your mercies are not bound
    By designs which cannot move,
But are measured in the realm
    Founded through Your steadfast love.
All distress shall pass me by,
When, by grace, You hear me cry.

# Psalm 7

*A Prayer for Deliverance*


O LORD, my God, my refuge sure,
  In Thee my hope is laid;
Before the looming veil of death,
  My soul is unafraid.

Though failures of my life abound,
  Thy mercy shall preserve;
And Thy redemptive gift of grace
  Is more than I deserve.

Arise, O LORD, and in Thy wrath
  Mete justice swift and smart;
Weigh righteousness against deceit,
  And spare the pure in heart.

For Thou art yet the sword and shield
  Before whom foes shall bend;
And those whom faith redeems shall sing
  Thy praises without end.

# Psalm 8

*A Hymn to God's Glory*

O LORD, our LORD, Thy majesty
    Is sung in all the earth;
Who hung the moon and stars in space,
And gave to us, Thy chosen race,
    From dust a noble birth.

How vast the heav'ns, how small are we,
    And yet we feel Thy care.
O who are we to own such grace,
To see Thy glory face to face,
    Thy goodness ev'rywhere?

All creatures bow beneath our feet;
    Through us their wants attend.
For life and love so freely giv'n,
May we preserve the gift of heav'n:
    Earth's love that knows no end!

# Psalm 9

*A Lament*

I will give thanks to God,
　Who wondrous gifts has given;
My heart delights to praise
　The Lord of earth and heaven.
God's justice never fails
　To rule with equity;
And measures of God's grace
　Are mine to set me free.

Our stronghold sure, O God,
　And shelter from oppression;
A constant source of strength
　Amid all tribulation.
For those who trust Thy name,
　Deliv'rance is their prize;
And those who seek Thy face
　Find favor in Thine eyes.

Be gracious, Lord, to me;
　How great my desolation;
A saving word from Thee
　My only consolation.
O lift me from the snares
　My wicked foes have laid;
And lead me through the mire
　Unscathed and unafraid.

Remember, Lord, how we
　Thy faithful blessings cherish;
Though death may hold us fast,
　Our hope shall never perish.
Arise, O God, in might
　Against unrighteous hands;
While earth shall fall to dust,
　God's kingdom ever stands.

# Psalm 10

*A Lament for Judgment Delayed*

LORD, why stand so far from me?
    Why desert in time of woe?
Hosts of evil gather 'round,
    Bait my steps where'er I go.
All ambitions of their hearts
    Are but for their selfish gain;
Base conceit shall count for naught;
    Lofty pride resound in vain.

All around, dark shadows fall;
    Godless hands with swords are raised;
God's great goodness meets with scorn,
    In its place, injustice praised.
Thou, O LORD, the Judge of all
    Shall reward our lives in kind:
Slaves to death, a grave is theirs,
    Faithful souls, redemption find.

# Psalm 11

*A Song of Trust*

The LORD to me a refuge is,
    When foes my faith deride;
Their fatal schemes I will not dread,
    If God is at my side.
The sparrow may to mountains flee
    To dodge the arrow's sting;
I to the LORD will turn for aid,
    And to God's promise cling.

God's temple is the universe,
    And heaven's arch a throne;
The good within God's courts rejoice,
    The wicked die alone.
The LORD delights in righteousness,
    And crowns pure deeds with grace;
To faithful hearts, with love alive,
    God turns a smiling face.

# Psalm 12

*A Lament*

LORD, hear our cry and send us aid,
    They press from ev'ry side;
The godless bask in vain deceit,
    And gloat in empty pride.

The words within their hearts are not
    The thoughts their lips express;
Their lies with honesty supplant,
    And wrong with righteousness.

As silver cast into the flame,
    Your promises are pure;
To all who show humility,
    Rich blessings shall endure.

# Psalm 13

*A Lament*

How long am I forgotten?
   Am I forever spurned?
O keep not from my sorrow
   Thy face in anger turned.
My heart is bowed with anguish,
   My foes inflict their pain;
While I no comfort merit;
   No hope for peace regain.

Around me hosts of evil
   Are quick to claim their prize;
If only death could free me,
   I pray Thee, close mine eyes.
But Thy great mercy ransoms
   My spirit from the grave;
Not even death can conquer
   Thy pow'r to bless and save.

# Psalm 14

*A Lament*

The foolish heart denies the LORD,
   And mocks divine decree;
The harvest of its work is vain,
   Its deeds bring misery.

From heav'n God looks upon our hearts
   To measure good and shame;
The wicked glory in themselves,
   While we exalt God's name.

They live their evil days as kings,
   Their scorn brings them to dust;
And from our shackles God will forge
   A scepter for the just.

# Psalm 15

*A Song of Trust*

LORD, who may in Thy temple dwell,
    Upon Thy holy hill abide?
Who shows forth love instead of hate,
    Humility in place of pride?

A blameless life help me to live,
    Free from contempt and selfish will;
When I through mortal frailness fail,
    God deigns by grace to love me still.

# Psalm 16

*A Song of Trust*

Preserve, O LORD, my trusting soul,
    Count me among the saints in light;
May I with them Your mercy gain,
    And rightful favor in Your sight.

How many are their schemes, O LORD,
    Who tempt me from the way I know;
Their gods of gold and strength and thought
    Confront me ev'ry step I go.

You, LORD, are my inheritance;
    Through generations I am heir
To righteousness in place of sin,
    Your grace to save me from despair.

At Your right hand I find delight
    In all the blessings kept in store;
The fullness of Your love, my joy;
    I praise Your glory evermore.

# Psalm 17

*A Prayer for Deliverance*


Hear, O LORD, my plea for justice,
    Listen to my heartfelt prayer;
In Thy just deliberation
    May I find redemption there.

Test my heart for its affliction,
    Purify my soul with fire;
Let my mortal tongue speak wisdom,
    Righteousness be my desire.

Keep me, LORD, in Thy protection,
    As the apple of Thine eye;
Shelter me beneath Thy shadow
    When my hour of death draws nigh.

In its wake send vindication;
    To its darkness, show Thy face;
Bring me to my resurrection
    Clothed in garments of Thy grace.

# Psalm 18

*A Psalm of Thanksgiving*

I love the LORD, who is my strength,
    My refuge in distress;
The object of unending praise,
    The source of righteousness.
When bonds of hell encompassed me,
    And death had set its snare;
I raised my tear-filled eyes to God,
    Who heard my plaintive prayer.

The oceans rolled and mountains shook
    At God's unbridled wrath,
And through the blazing holocaust
    God laid for me a path.
While evil foes God judged unfit
    And cast into the flame,
The righteous danced across the coals
    To praise God's holy name.

What god is there except the LORD,
    Whose way is perfect peace;
Whose justice is forever sure,
    Whose love will never cease?
May those who keep their faith in God
    Seek righteousness always;
And to the promise of God's grace
    Respond with songs of praise.

# Psalm 19

*A Hymn to God: Creator*


The heav'ns unfold Your glory, LORD,
    In ev'ry realm of space,
The outmost bounds of all that is
    Resound Your wondrous grace.
Succeeding days to day confess,
    And nights to night record
In words, beyond our sense to hear,
    The greatness of the LORD.

The earth's imagined cornerstones
    Acclaim with joy their Source,
Who sets the gleaming stars ablaze,
    And gives the sun its course.
In ev'ry place within the sphere
    Your craft is ever found;
Majestic mountains, seas, and skies
    With ordered might resound.

Your Word is sure and perfect still
    A source of light and life;
Your Law is right and reason-filled,
    Your peace, the end of strife.
Your everlasting truth and love
    Can scarce be fully told;
More sweet than honey from the comb,
    More precious yet than gold.

You know the secrets of our hearts,
    But deign to love us here;
Preserved from pride and self-conceit,
    We meet You without fear.
May all the words our tongues shall speak,
    And all our thoughts in store
Find grace with You, Redeemer, Rock,
    Now and for evermore.

# Psalm 20

*A Prayer for Victory*

LORD, hear our supplication,
    For trouble is at hand;
And be to us a strong defense
    When foes against us stand.
Remember then our tributes,
    Each sacrifice to Thee;
Accept them as Thine honor due,
    And bring us victory.

The LORD shall with a victor's crown
    Adorn the servant's head;
God's foes proclaim their own conceit,
    I praise my LORD instead.
Their pride falls to destruction,
    Yet I am ever brave,
Assured God's purpose is to judge,
    God's mercy is to save.

# Psalm 21

*A Psalm of Praise for Deliverance*

To Thine unequalled strength, O LORD,
    Thy chosen ones aspire;
Bring to the just sure victory,
    And grant their hearts' desire.

The rulers of the LORD's elect
    Wear crowns of finest gold;
Their lives once empty, now through faith
    Shall burst with wealth untold.

To those whom honor shall bestow
    On Thee, shall honor come;
And those in whom goodwill abides
    In Thee will find a home.

In wrath our enemies will fall,
    Thine arm puts them to flight;
We gain our blessings by Thy grace,
    And vict'ry through Thy might.

# Psalm 22a

*Forsaken of God: A Lament*


My God, am I forsaken?
  Why turn from me Thine eyes?
Why cease to feel my anguish,
  Or hear my plaintive cries?
The ones who came before me
  Found merit for their trust;
While I, despised, tormented,
  Am cast into the dust.

With scorn my foes deride me,
  Their taunts my faith would move;
Yet firm is my conviction,
  Deep-rooted in Thy love.
My God, my sure salvation,
  Be near me all my days;
Whatever may befall me,
  Remain my strength always.

# Psalm 22b

*A Psalm of Praise*

I come with praise before the LORD,
    Release me from all strife;
The poor will feast at tables full
    And find eternal life.

The far-flung corners of the earth
    Shall turn to God and sing;
And nations of the world shall rise
    To hail the LORD as King.

The mighty on their knees will bow;
    As mortals, they discern
That, as from dust God gave them breath,
    To dust they shall return.

Descendants of the coming years
    Who walk the paths well trod
Will sing to children yet unborn
    The mighty acts of God.

# Psalm 23

*A Song of Trust*


As faithful shepherds tend their flocks,
    So God will care for me;
And from God's store of grace my needs
    Are met abundantly.
In pastures green, by waters still,
    My soul new life doth take;
And in the paths of righteousness
    I follow, for God's sake.

When death surrounds I will not fear,
    God's strength dispels my dread;
I hold God's blessing in my heart
    And face my fear instead.
For as a lamb, my comfort rests
    Upon the Shepherd's rod,
To bring me home, where'er I stray
    Into the fold of God.

A bounteous feast for me is placed
    In the presence of my foes;
My head with oil the LORD anoints,
    My cup with grace o'erflows.
The loving-kindness of the LORD
    Is mine for all my days;
And in God's house for evermore
    I'll join the songs of praise.

# Psalm 24

*A Psalm to the King of Glory*

LORD, all creation with Thy name resounds,
    And all who dwell within earth's ample bounds;
Ever above the seas have mountains stood,
    Planted by Thy design upon the flood.

Who shall to Zion's sacred heights ascend?
    Within God's house, whom shall the LORD defend?
The true, the meek, the righteous and the pure
    Shall in God's courts of blessing long endure.

Lift high your heads, O gates, before the LORD!
    Unfold to greet our God with one accord!
Break free the bonds which bind you to your walls!
    Welcome the mighty God, the LORD of all!

Lift up your heads, O ancient doors, and give
    Passage unbarred to God, in whom we live;
Who is this God, who merits such delight?
    The LORD Almighty, crowned in glory bright!

# Psalm 25

*A Prayer for Guidance*


To Thee, O LORD, I lift my soul,
    In Thee, O God, I trust;
Let vanity be put to shame,
    And languish in the dust.

Make me to know Thy paths, O God,
    And lead me in Thy way;
To learn Thy saving truth my heart
    shall meditate each day.

The LORD is goodness, truth, and love,
    God's path the saints have trod;
And children of the covenant
    Still walk beside their God.

Be mindful of Thy mercy, LORD,
    Thy love from ages past;
Forgive the weakness of my youth
    And bring me home at last.

# Psalm 26

*A Prayer for Deliverance*


Be Thou my judge, O LORD, my God,
　　For I have walked among the just;
With confidence, I shall not fall,
　　For always Thou hast been my trust.

Test me, O LORD, before Thy sight;
　　The secrets of my heart reveal;
And for the wrongs which mar my cause,
　　To Thy great mercy, I appeal.

I flee from empty boasts of pride,
　　And shun the dismal haunts of woe;
Their evil threats, my path would spurn;
　　Thy truth, my light, where'er I go.

O God, I love Thy holy house,
　　Where justice clothed in love resides;
The lure of earth cannot corrupt
　　The soul which in Thy grace abides.

# Psalm 27

*A Psalm of Confidence*

God, my light and my salvation,
    In whose strength my hope is laid;
Confident in my salvation,
    I shall never be afraid.
Evil hosts may rise against me,
    Wars distress, and flesh decays;
Yet the cruelest death imagined
    But begins my song of praise.

Shelter me within the haven
    Of Thy house all time to come;
On the rock of Thy protection,
    Let me safely find a home.
Lift me high above the legions
    Who would rail against Thy word;
O'er the tumult of division
    Make my cry for peace be heard.

When my trust is disappointed,
    Faith confronted with disdain;
Friend and foe defeat my purpose,
    Even then wilt Thou sustain.
Had I not with eyes believing
    Seen the goodness of Thy face,
Never could I taste Thy pleasure,
    Nor await Thy saving grace.

# Psalm 28

*A Prayer for Deliverance*


O LORD, my strength, to Thee I cry;
   ignore my plea, and I shall die.
My soul would perish in the grave,
   Except for Thy desire to save.

Fearful, I pour my heart to Thee.
   Answer with grace, humility;
For my transgressions, guilt is mine;
   Yet is redemption wholly Thine.

Thanks be to Thee, who hears my prayer;
   With me Thy joy and favor share;
My strength, my shield, my health always;
   Forever let me sing Thy praise!

# Psalm 29

*A Hymn*

All on earth and all in heaven,
    Raise to God a song on high;
Strength unmeasured, love unbounded,
    God alone we glorify.
At God's voice the clouds assemble,
    Thunder roars and torrents fall;
Earth shall quake before God's presence,
    Mountains tremble at God's call.

Trees shall bow in awe and wonder,
    Bend their branches to the ground;
From God's lips one word in anger
    Wreaks destruction all around.
But the Word which sets in motion
    Such travails can make them cease;
That same voice which tumult beckons
    In a gentler breath speaks peace.

# Psalm 30

*Thanksgiving for Healing*

Sing to God, that all may hear you!
  God, whose arms can lift and save;
By Thy healing touch, revive us,
  Life restore beyond the grave.
Praise we now our sure salvation,
  God, the holy One above,
End the night so dimmed by anguish,
  With the sunrise of Thy love.

God, whose wrath we more than merit;
  God, whose grace we cannot earn;
When the pride of human nature
  From Thy way tempts us to turn;
Then we cry to Thee for mercy,
  "Can the tomb repeat Thy praise?"
Through Thy goodness, yet redeem us,
  Make us faithful all our days.

Change our sorrow to rejoicing,
  Clothe with gladness all despair;
Cause unsteady feet that stumble
  Now to dance beneath Thy care.
Dry the tears we shed in mourning,
  Give us steadfast hope always;
Fill our hearts with expectation,
  And our songs with thanks and praise.

# Psalm 31a

*A Psalm of Trust*

O LORD, in whom my soul confides;
    My refuge sure amid the strife;
O let me not in shame reside,
    But through Thy grace reclaim my life.

Be Thou my rock, my sure defense,
    My fortress which no force can break;
Remain my guide, and lead me forth
    To praise Thee for Thy mercy's sake.

My life, my days, are in Thy hand,
    Naught can the threat of death remove;
Turn now to me Thy shining face,
    And save me through Thy steadfast love.

# Psalm 31b

*A Cry for Help*

Be gracious, Lord, for I, in anguish,
    Your heartfelt mercy now implore;
The very heart within me planted
    Can bear its grief alone no more.

My eyes have wasted all their crying,
    My life with sorrow melts away;
The loving thoughts of those around me
    In scorn and mem'ry fast decay.

Amid the pain of their denial,
    I come, O Lord, to You for grace;
My trust is in Your steadfast mercy,
    I glory in Your smiling face.

# Psalm 32

*A Psalm of Thanksgiving*

How blest those whose transgressions
    The LORD forgives through grace;
Who, as the heirs of mercy,
    Find peace before God's face.
The heart with guilt so heavy
    It bends to bear the strain
Can yield God its affliction
    And claim its strength again.

The LORD with absolution
    Will greet the penitent,
And send the dawn of mercy
    Before the night is spent.
God to the meek and lowly
    A hiding place shall be;
In danger, their salvation;
    From sin, their liberty.

Instill in me Your wisdom,
    Instruct me in Your ways;
Grant but a word of pardon
    And I respond with praise.
God's steadfast love surrounds me,
    And doubts shall soon depart;
Redeemed, my soul rejoices,
    And gladness fills my heart.

# Psalm 33

*Praise to God: Creator*

Rejoice, ye righteous, in the LORD,
    In song your voices raise;
Awake the harp and psaltery,
    Lift up God's name in praise!
For by God's word the heavens
    Were hung; the sea, the land,
And all that fill the firmament
    Were made at God's command.

Let ev'ry nation of the earth
    Unite with one accord,
And humbly lay their heartfelt prayers
    In awe before the LORD.
How happy are God's children,
    How blest God's chosen heirs,
For surely an inheritance
    Of glory shall be theirs!

Behold, God's ever-watchful eye
    Sees through our dark despair;
The arms of Grace encircle us
    With strong, yet tender care;
The hope of countless ages,
    Who sets at peace our fears,
God's mercy and compassion
    Shall follow all our years.

# Psalm 34

*A Psalm of Thanksgiving*

Unto the LORD my praise I sing,
    God's goodness ever bless;
The proud convictions of my soul
    Speak of God's righteousness.

Come, magnify the LORD with me!
    Together bring God praise,
Whose presence overcomes all fear,
    And glory lights our days.

O taste and see, the LORD is good!
    How blest are they who place
Reliance on God's steadfast love,
    And trust God's saving grace.

So great the trials of the just,
    Yet greater is God's will,
That from the threat'ning chill of death
    God's truth redeems us still.

# Psalm 35

*A Prayer for Help*

Defend my cause, O LORD, with them
    Whose might against my life contend;
To their assault, confusion bring;
    To Thine elect, salvation send.

Confound and shame all evil ways
    Of those who work iniquity;
Their limbs entangle in the snare
    Which craftily they set for me.

I cannot plead God's wrath on them
    Unless I, too, Thy judgment own;
Let my desire for righteousness
    Keep me from standing trial alone.

They shout for joy, who in God's courts
    will find an everlasting home;
God's justice and prosperity
    Shall ever be my joyful song.

# Psalm 36

*A Song of God's Goodness*

Thy gifts, O LORD, surpass the heav'ns,
    Thy faithfulness, the clouds above;
How matchless is Thy righteousness;
    How dear is Thy redeeming love.

Beneath the shadow of Thy wings,
    Thy people banquet at Thy board;
They drink the cup of pure delights
    And taste the pleasure of the LORD.

God is the wellspring of my life,
    And in God's light, I light shall see;
The pure of heart true favor find,
    And in God's law their liberty.

# Psalm 37

*A Wisdom Psalm*

Fret not the crowds of evil,
    The fortunes they amass;
Like blossoms they shall wither,
    And fade as new-mown grass.
But trust the LORD, whose goodness
    Your faithfulness inspires;
Delight in God, whose graciousness
    Fulfills your heart's desires.

Commit your ways unto the LORD,
    Who vindication brings;
The soul that patiently attends,
    A song of vict'ry sings.
God's foes shall fall in anguish,
    The meek possess the land;
While they as by the sword are drawn,
    We feast from God's own hand.

Though hosts may deal affliction,
    The LORD our strength shall be;
God's might shall burst the nets they cast
    And set the captives free.
Salvation is the promise
    The LORD preserves in store
For those who live in goodness,
    And trust God evermore.

# Psalm 38

*A Prayer for Mercy*


O LORD, I pray, judge not my cause
　　In wrath, though I transgress Thy laws;
The burden of my guilt would take
　　My life, but for Thy mercy's sake.

I ache in spirit, heart, and mind,
　　For peace in God alone I find;
My tongue too long refused to share
　　The pain my sins have brought to bear.

The anguish of unrighteousness
　　To Thy good grace I now confess;
The tears I shed for selfish gain
　　Are powerless to cleanse the stain.

To Thee, O God, in hope I pray
　　That Thou, who hath shown me the way
Will patience and devotion send
　　That I may follow to the end.

# Psalm 39

*A Lament in Times of Trouble*

My words a wicked tongue subdued,
    They passed without a sound;
In silence I withheld the grief
    Which compassed me around.

How long, O LORD, before my end?
    How many are the days
Until my frail and feeble soul
    Shall see Thy courts of praise?

The things of earth are vanity;
    They pass before the night;
False treasures cast a tempting gleam,
    Then fade before our sight.

My hope, my confidence, my faith,
    O God, I rest in Thee;
A stranger, grant me strength to dwell,
    With Thee eternally.

# Psalm 40

*A Song of Delight in the LORD*

With patient hope I waited
    For God to hear my plea;
And from the depths of my despair,
    God's arm uplifted me.
My feet are set upon the rock,
    Where none can make me fall;
My mouth is filled with songs of praise
    To God, my all in all.

How blest the truly faithful,
    Who trust the LORD of Hosts;
They set no store in empty pride,
    No hope in idle boasts.
The treasures of our fragile minds,
    False gods of wealth and fame,
Are naught to those who know God's works,
    And kneel before God's name.

The ancient cost of pardon
    Thy Law no more requires;
A willing and compliant heart
    Fulfills the LORD's desire.
I always sing of God's goodwill,
    God's praise is my delight:
My joy, to know this humble life
    Is pleasing in God's sight.

I celebrate the goodness
    Which God has shown to me:
The patience to endure my cross,
    The grace to set me free.
The gifts I truly prize are such
    That earth cannot remove:
God's favor for my faithfulness,
    And mercy for my love.

# Psalm 41

*A Prayer for Mercy*

O blest are they who in their love
    Compassion hold for those in need;
For they shall find, when faced by foes,
    The LORD is their defense indeed.

When all the evils earth can dream
    Are cast on me, my faith to break;
Their rage I temper through God's grace,
    And bear them boldly for God's sake.

The hands which shared my broken bread,
    My love with their deceit repaid;
And friends whose trust I counted mine
    Have left me wounded and betrayed.

To me, O LORD, in mercy turn;
    Thy favor is a shield to me.
My mouth shall sing the victor's song,
    My tongue declare my love for Thee.

# Book II

## Psalm 42

*A Prayer for Deliverance*

Cool streams a breathless deer desires.
    So longs my soul, O God, for Thee;
I thirst to see Thy face, O God,
    My heart, Thy habitation be.

"Where is your God?" they ask of me,
    When tears have been my only food;
How long, O LORD, till doubts dispel
    My tattered mem'ries of Thy good?

Deep calls to deep, and oceans roar,
    Their thunder my destruction brings;
Yet steadfast love my hope sustains,
    My tongue divine assurance sings.

Why grieves my soul and stirs my heart
    When shallow threats of death assail?
My hope, my rock, my sure defense
    Remains the God of Israel.

# Psalm 43

*A Prayer for God's Presence*


Pronounce for me Your judgment, God,
    Defend my righteous part
Against the vain, ungodly foes
    Who would corrupt my heart.
For You, O God, have been my strength
    In generations past;
Though I may doubt, Your presence will
    Protect me to the last.

Send out Your light and shining truth
    To lead the faithful home;
May I within Your holy hill
    Delight for years to come.
And in Your courts of joy and peace
    I will to You always
Repay the goodness poured on me
    With songs of thanks and praise.

# Psalm 44

*A Prayer for Deliverance*

Your goodness, LORD, and wondrous deeds
    Across the years are told.
To generations yet unborn
    By faithful hearts of old
By Your own hand the nations fell,
    New lands did come to be;
Through Your own might were foes subdued,
    And by Your Word set free.

I cannot trust in sword and shield,
    Except the LORD will guide;
Nor can I claim the victory,
    But You are at my side.
O help me, God, not to forget
    Your goodness shown to me;
Lest in the hour I need You most,
    I, too, forgotten be.

God knows the secrets of my heart,
    The weakness of my will;
I cry, "Awake!" God does not sleep,
    Yet deigns to love me still.
So build my hope and confidence
    That none can dare remove;
Make me as steadfast in my faith
    As Thou art in Thy love.

# Psalm 45a

*A Psalm of Joy*

How our hearts with joy abound,
  With Thy beauty all around;
Words are feeble to express
  Thy great love and righteousness.

Fairer still than human frame,
  Ever to our eyes the same;
Steadfast love shines from Thy face;
  From Thy lips flow words of grace.

Thine the scepter, Thine the throne;
  Thou to us art God alone;
Vast the mercies to us giv'n:
  Wealth of earth, and joy of heav'n.

# Psalm 45b

*A Song of God's Glory*

Sons and daughters of the earth,
    Set your minds beyond your kin;
Great the LORD, and great the courts
    God's elect may enter in.
Glorious gifts, for mercy's sake,
    We are chosen to partake.

Come with joy and highest praise
    Into God's most sacred hall;
Let your song of praise proclaim:
    God alone is LORD of all.
Generations yet to be
    Shall declare their love for Thee.

# Psalm 46

*A Psalm of Trust*


God, our strength and mighty fortress,
    God, our refuge in distress;
God, whose promise is deliv'rance,
    God, whose law is righteousness;
Though the earth with fear may tremble,
    None can shake Thy faithfulness.

In the city of the Holy,
    Rivers flow and streams run pure;
Where the LORD abides in splendor,
    There Thy people dwell secure.
In their hearts, Thy love will flourish,
    Through their faith, Thy word endure.

Come, behold God's matchless wonders,
    See the bounty of God's hand;
Gifts beyond our expectations,
    Works too great to understand.
Sound God's might in songs of glory
    Sung to earth's most distant land.

# Psalm 47

*A Psalm of Praise*

Clap your hands, O faithful people!
    Shout to God a song of praise!
From the dust of conquered nations,
    God a realm of grace shall raise.
In appointed courts of glory
    Faithful to God's name always,
    May we prosper all our days.

With a shout, and blast of trumpet,
    God shall mount a throne on high;
Let our praise, as finest incense,
    Rise to meet God in the sky.
Fill the world with glad rejoicing,
    Heav'n shall sing, and earth reply,
    All God's works to glorify.

Let your hearts be filled with gladness,
    As the LORD your life shall bless;
Live as heirs of God's great justice,
    Wear the cloak of righteousness.
God will grant us earth's dominion,
    All things good, and nothing less,
    For our gift of faithfulness.

# Psalm 48

*A Song of Security*

How great is the LORD and worthy of praise,
Whose glory above Mount Zion displays!
In light of Thy splendor our cities are dust;
Eternal our refuge, unquestioned our trust.

The rulers of earth are shaken with fright,
When Thou in Thy wrath appear in their sight;
But we as Thy chosen have witnessed Thy heart,
And at its remembrance, all fears soon depart.

The far-fashioned bounds of earth lift their voice,
And for Thy goodwill, the mountains rejoice;
Thy righteousness follows the course of our days;
Whatever our pathway, our Guide for always.

# Psalm 49

*A Wisdom Psalm*


Hear this, all folk together,
    Of low and high degree;
Both rich and poor, speak wisdom,
    And ponder faithfully
How God alone the ransom
    For mortal life can pay,
How mortal wealth, like shadows,
    Fades with the dying day.

All life in time must perish,
    The grave becomes its bed;
False pride and vain ambition
    Decay among the dead.
How foolish they whose fortunes
    In earthly molds are cast;
While human love dies with them,
    The love of God will last.

The glimmer of our treasure
    Will not salvation win,
For God shall judge our glory
    By light that shines within.
The joy we hold sufficient
    Is slight before God's eyes,
For naught on earth can capture
    The taste of Paradise.

*The Psalter for Christian Worship*

# Psalm 50

*A Psalm of Judgment*

The Mighty One, the LORD of Hosts,
    Speaks and the world obeys;
From dawn until the setting sun,
    God's wonder earth displays.
The perfect beauty all around
    From Zion's height shines forth;
And stars across the firmament
    So brightly beam their worth.

God comes, not with a silent form,
    But riding on the winds;
Before God's face, the raging storm
    Its blasts of thunder sends
All hail the Judge, in bold array,
    Who weighs our righteousness
Against all sin, and with whose grace
    Deigns faithful hearts to bless.

The heav'ns declare Thy justice, LORD,
    As endless as the sky;
Against the taunts of disbelief,
    Our God will testify.
Receive my heartfelt gift of thanks
    As honor to Thy might;
Refresh my faith with each new day;
    Protect me through the night.

# Psalm 51

*A Psalm of Penitence*

Have mercy, LORD, according to
    The measure of Thy love;
Blot out my sin, and from my heart
    All wickedness remove.

The failings of my deeds and thoughts
    Are ever in my sight;
Release me from the path of death,
    And set my course aright.

Into my secret heart send truth,
    Let wisdom in me grow;
O wash the evil from my hands,
    And make me pure as snow.

A clean and upright heart, O LORD,
    Exchange for mine of stone;
Thy Holy Spirit meld with mine,
    And leave me not alone.

A contrite heart is Thy desire,
    My offering, the same;
My lips unlatch, my mouth engage
    Thy praises to proclaim.

# Psalm 52

*A Psalm of Judgment*


Why your boast, O wicked mortals?
    Why your pride in vain deceit?
All your efforts work their malice,
    God's true causes to defeat.
Like a sword, your evil cunning
    Cuts the righteous to the core;
But the LORD rejects deception,
    And endures your hate no more.

Then the righteous shall with laughter
    Celebrate your earned demise;
Raise new virtue from your ashes,
    Speak the truth above your lies.
By God's justice shall the faithful
    Claim your loss as their own gain;
Evermore God's praises render,
    Ever in God's house remain.

# Psalm 53

*A Song of Human Folly*

How the foolish in their hearts
    Can the law of God deny!
All their evil deeds are vain,
    Every oath a vicious lie.
God from heav'n the earth surveys,
    All must pass before God's eyes;
Is there one the LORD calls good?
    Is there none God counts as wise?

All have turned in their conceit
    To their own innate desires;
Faith has fled the doubt of scorn,
    Selfish love with hate conspires.
But the dreadful day shall come,
    Retribution for their wrongs;
Then shall all our cries of grief
    Be transformed to joyful songs.

# Psalm 54

*A Lament*


O save me, God, and hear my cry;
    My prayer to Thee ascends;
And vindicate me by Thy might;
    On Thee, my hope depends.

Thou, LORD, my help shall ever be,
    Though evil pow'rs assail;
From their designs, my life redeem
    Through grace which cannot fail.

My sacrifice I offer Thee,
    As thanks for all Thy grace;
Let me so live, that I in death
    May greet Thee face to face.

# Psalm 55

*A Lament*

Give ear, O LORD, unto my prayer;
    Hide not Thyself from my distress.
The sound of hatred fills the air,
    The fears of death upon me press.

O that my wings were like a dove,
    I'd fly away and be at rest,
Far from the raging war remove
    To prosper in the wilderness.

My foes I counted once as friends
    Now break the heart that held them dear;
They work deceit to gain their ends,
    And fellowship confound with fear.

I cast my burden on the LORD,
    And through my life God will sustain;
The righteous praise with one accord,
    And in God's endless love remain.

# Psalm 56

*A Prayer for Deliverance*

Be gracious unto me, O LORD,
    For great is my distress;
At ev'ry hand, Thy foes conspire
    An end to righteousness.

When bound by fear of their assault,
    I set my faith in Thee;
If Thee I trust with spirit sure,
    What harm can come to me?

Thou, LORD, hath seen what I endure,
    Each step along the way;
O keep a record of my tears
    And turn each threat away.

My faithful vows I must perform,
    For God, whose Word I praise;
That Thou to me might faithful be
    Throughout my future days.

# Psalm 57

*A Prayer for Deliverance*


Be merciful to me, O God,
    I trust alone in Thee;
That in the shadow of Thy wings
    My resting place might be.
Send forth Thy sure salvation
    To me before I fall,
And for Thy favor I shall claim
    Thee as the LORD of all.

My heart is steadfast in its faith
    That Thou will hear my voice;
With confidence, my soul, awake,
    And in Thy truth rejoice!
Thy love to me surpasses
    My talents to proclaim;
Yet with my life I celebrate
    The glories of Thy name.

# Psalm 58

*A Lament*

Those who judge the deeds of others
 Must be led by righteousness;
Lest the verdict of injustice
 Their own evil works express.
Can the guilty find them guilty,
 Who by grace should pardon see?
Can they bind the poor in shackles
 Who by right should be set free?

From their birth the hosts of evil
 At the just, in anger rave;
Their assaults will sting but vanish,
 Justice reigns beyond the grave.
Though like thorns their threats may pierce us,
 They those same thorns shall embrace;
God, who shall decree their sentence,
 Rescues us through boundless grace.

# Psalm 59

*A Prayer for Deliverance*

Deliver me from all my foes,
    Subdue the hands my blood would shed;
Let rampant pride with grace be bound,
    And starving hate with love be fed.

O Lord of hosts, I Thee implore,
    Rise to my aid, and Thou shall see
The mockery and bitter scorn
    I through my faith endure for Thee.

Thou, God, my fortress and my strength,
    All foul profanity remove;
Let lies with truth be overcome,
    And empty threats with words of love.

My song, O Lord, shall ever be
    Of faith and justice all my days;
Since Thou the vict'ry hath assured,
    Who else stands worthy of my praise?

# Psalm 60

*A Prayer for Deliverance*

The Lord in wrath, and rightly so,
    Should us abandon to our sin;
Yet, grace such anger can subdue,
    And bring us to God's fold again.

The earth may shake, the mountains fall,
    The desert plain apart be rent;
No vict'ry comes but by God's hand;
    No peace without the Lord's consent.

What help have we without God's aid
    To strengthen us against the sword?
Our faith is in God's promise laid,
    Our hope is anchored in God's Word.

# Psalm 61

*A Prayer for Protection*

Hear my cry, O Rock of Ages,
    To my earnest prayer, give ear;
Grant me refuge from disaster,
    Confidence to vanquish fear.

Thou, O God, hast heard my bidding,
    Once delivered, yet the same;
Thou will ne'er forget the promise
    Giv'n to all who fear Thy name.

In Thy tent afford protection,
    Shelter me beneath Thy wing;
Let my tongue, filled with Thy praises,
    In Thy courts forever sing.

# Psalm 62

*A Song of Trust*

My soul, O God, in silence waits;
    My hope secure without a sound;
The LORD's my refuge and my rock,
    In whom the joys of life abound.

I set my trust in Thee beyond
    The futile boasts of mortal pride;
With confidence I hold Thy prize,
    And cast dishonest claims aside.

Into my silence, Thou hast said
    That goodness rests with Thee above;
The recompense for my delight,
    A share of Thine unfailing love.

# Psalm 63

*A Lament*

O God, my God, with eagerness
    I long to see Your face;
Lost in a dry and barren land,
    I thirst to taste Your grace.

Your endless mercies, LORD, are mine
    As Your appointed heir;
Your steadfast love throughout my life
    Is joy beyond compare.

My soul has feasted at Your board,
    Your glories fill my sight;
I spend my waking hours in praise,
    And pray my thoughts at night.

Throughout my life You are my help,
    My soul is bold to sing;
And after death, I'll rest beneath
    The shadow of Your wing.

# Psalm 64

*A Prayer for Deliverance*

Before the savage threat of foes,
    My earnest prayers attend;
From their most sinister intent,
    O LORD, Your child defend.

Their tongues, like swords, assail my faith
    With bitter words of woe;
My path is set with cunning snares
    No matter where I go.

LORD, You alone, their vengeance turn,
    And justice will impart;
In righteousness, I shall rejoice,
    And hold You in my heart.

# Psalm 65

*A Psalm of Thanksgiving*

The praises of Zion, O God, are Thy due;
Thy mercies are countless, our merits are few;
The weight of transgressions Thy grace will remove,
And give life we cherish, redeemed by Thy love.

Thy strength has established the sea and the plain;
Each day all creation Thy praise sings again;
The God of salvation, our hope for always,
A shelter in darkness, the light of our days.

The earth's endless bounty, LORD, let us preserve;
Its richness and splendor we less than deserve;
The cycle of seasons gives sense to the year,
An autumn for harvest, a springtime of cheer!

# Psalm 66a

*A Psalm of Thanksgiving*

Make a joyful noise to God!
    All creation worships Thee!
Great Thy wonders here displayed,
    Unexcelled in majesty.
Glorious is Thy sacred name,
    Ages old, yet still the same.

Come and see what God has done:
    Great the blessings to the just;
Walked the chosen through the sea;
    Brought their enemies to dust.
Let us lift a thankful voice
    For Thy mercies, and rejoice!

Bless the LORD, our refuge sure;
    Let your song of praise be heard!
By whose justice, we are tried;
    By whose grace, our guilt deferred.
When our life its end shall see,
    Bring us home to dwell with Thee.

# Psalm 66b

*A Prayer for Help*


O bless the LORD, ye peoples, all,
    Let songs of praise resound!
For in the midst of our distress,
    God's presence can be found.

The ancient law required of me
    Burnt off'rings for my part;
But as a nobler sacrifice,
    I offer God my heart.

Would that the world in ev'ry place
    Knew God as I have known;
God shares my joy, and in my grief
    Will leave me not alone.

Bless God, all you who would the lies
    Of sinful lips disprove;
With truth God shall sustain your way,
    Your life with steadfast love.

# Psalm 67

*A Psalm of Thanksgiving*

God of mercy and compassion,
    LORD of love, redeeming grace;
Let the brightness of Your glory
    Shine upon us in this place.
Show all nations Your salvation,
    End our dark, long-suff'ring days;
Cause our hearts with joy to greet You;
    Fill the earth with songs of praise!

Sing with joy, the LORD is coming!
    God with us, Immanuel,
Brings in triumph our salvation,
    Death shall die, and life prevail.
In the wisdom of God's justice
    Righteousness shall conquer scorn;
On God's head, the crown of nations;
    In God's heart, a crown of thorns.

Come, Almighty, now and bless us,
    Your great covenant renew;
May creation yield its increase,
    Find its greatest gift in You.
Ev'ry tongue shall call You blessed,
    Ev'ry voice a welcome bring
To the Word of God incarnate;
    Earth shall bow, and heaven sing!

# Psalm 68

*A Psalm of Celebration*


Arise, LORD, and hasten,
All woe, swiftly chasten,
As smoke in the whirlwind
    So drive it away!
While malice shall perish,
Thy goodness we cherish,
With joy shall the righteous
    All sadness betray!

Sing praise to God only,
Ye poor folk, and lonely,
For out of compassion
    God cares for us all.
The blessings we savor
Are ours by God's favor;
Whose goodness, like raindrops,
    On deserts shall fall.

All realms of creation
Now sing with elation
Their praise to the Maker
    Of earth and of sea.
The heav'ns, in their glory,
Resound with the story
Of God's matchless power
    All ages to be.

Ascribe to God wonder,
Whose voice, like the thunder,
Can shatter the stillness
    And call us to praise;
Whose Spirit life gave us,
Whose mercy can save us,
The Source of our being,
    The Joy of our days!

# Psalm 69

*A Psalm of Deliverance*


Save me, O God, lest I should perish;
    None else can raise me from the mire;
My only hope for sure salvation
    Is that my life is Thy desire.
My throat is parched as desert sod,
    And dimming eyes await my God.

Countless are those who hate me sorely;
    Mighty are they who would destroy!
Let bitter scorn not spoil my honor,
    Nor vain contention steal my joy.
Since for my faith, I suffer shame,
    Save me, O LORD, I trust Thy name.

My hope, Thy promise to redeem me,
    Shall be a shield against despair;
Who can assail me with a vengeance,
    If at my side, Thou, LORD, art there?
Make evil fail in its deceit,
    Swallow its pride in self-defeat.

O could I sing Thy praise forever,
    Offer my thanks to Thee aright;
More than a sacrifice of riches,
    A grateful heart is Thy delight!
Let earth and heav'n, as with one voice,
    Sound forth Thy glory, and rejoice!

# Psalm 70

*A Prayer for Deliverance*

May the LORD be pleased to save me;
  Hasten, for the time draws near,
When the vicious hosts of evil
  At my shattered camp appear.

Turn them back, the proud, the mighty,
  Let them fall in their conceit;
Bid the foes that would o'erwhelm me
  Trace their path in swift retreat.

I alone cannot withstand them,
  God, my strength, be at my side;
In Thy courts, secure, protected,
  Soon, O LORD, let me abide.

*The Psalter for Christian Worship*

# Psalm 71

*A Prayer for Deliverance*

In Thee, O LORD, I put my trust;
    Preserve from fear and shame
The righteous servant in distress
    Who calls upon Thy name.

For from the moment of my birth
    Through my allotted days,
I shall not waver in my trust,
    Or cease to sing Thy praise.

O God, be never far from me,
    Thy favor I implore;
I'll hope in Thee all time to come,
    And praise Thee evermore.

# Psalm 72

*A Prayer for Those Who Govern*

Grant justice, LORD, to those who rule;
    Let righteousness compel their hand;
Their courts shall bear prosperity,
    And serve the poor throughout the land.
O LORD, our cause defend;
Deliv'rance quickly send
    To those who, bound in chains
    Of greed and selfish gains,
Submit themselves to Thy command.

As long as sun and stars of space
    Walk their divine-appointed round;
Long as endures our feeble race,
    The blessings of the LORD abound.
Like rains that feed the field,
Our LORD to us will yield
    The bounty and the peace
    Which God will never cease
To shower where true faith is found.

God's righteousness extends to all
    Who seek assurance in distress;
The weak who in their anguish bend
    When hate and violence oppress.
As golden sheaves of grain,
God's harvest we remain;
    All praise to God above!
    Who crowns our life with love,
O bless God's name forever.

# Book III

## Psalm 73

*A Wisdom Psalm*


The LORD is surely good
    To those whose hearts are pure;
To those upright, who in God's sight
    Are just, the path is sure.
But all along my way,
    The tempter's charm I see;
LORD, cast aside ambitious pride,
    And keep me true to Thee.

The proud with self are clothed,
    And greed their will commands;
Vain hearts are rent with discontent
    That God their praise demands.
As slaves they hold us fast,
    And all goodwill oppress;
They use deceit for our defeat,
    And wrong for righteousness.

I know my weakness, LORD,
    The ease with which I fall;
At Thy right hand, I long to stand
    And claim Thee LORD of all!
What hope have I in earth,
    Or glory yet to be?
My flesh is frail, my heart may fail,
    But not my love for Thee.

# Psalm 74

*A Lament*

Lord, why do You cast us off?
    Why dismiss us to the dead?
Why consume with fiery rage
    Pastures where Your sheep once fed?
When Your temple, like Your Law,
    Is by hateful hands destroyed,
Can we not but mourn the loss
    Of Your peace we once enjoyed?

Filled with wonder, we recall
    Mercies far beyond our dreams;
Seas did part to yield a path;
    Arid fields were fed with streams.
Life You gave where life was lost,
    Gardens in the wilderness;
Have we so refused to love,
    That You, too, refuse to bless?

Know our grief, and help us, Lord,
    To regain our favored place;
Bring us home into Your fold;
    Reinstate us in Thy grace.
Your great promise to redeem
    Made to us, may we reclaim;
Make those worthy of Your love,
    Who in faith Your love proclaim.

# Psalm 75

*Thanksgiving for God's Justice*

We give Thee thanks, O God,
    For all Thy goodness shown us;
By whose design creates,
    And by whose Name doth own us.
To judge with equity,
    God shall appoint a term;
Though earth's dominions shake,
    Its pillars shall stand firm.

The proud will boast no more,
    Nor lift their horns in splendor;
When hosts of God's elect
    Will vanquish the pretender.
All arrogance will fall,
    And in its place is love;
For who in earth compares
    With God, who reigns above?

God's justice, swift and sure,
    To all is equal measure;
The mighty and the meek
    Must answer God's displeasure.
Each one must from the cup
    Of judgment taste their strife:
The wicked, bitter gall;
    The good, eternal life.

# Psalm 76

*A Song of God's Victory*

Throughout the earth, O LORD,
    Is Thy dominion spread;
Jerusalem Thy temple holds,
    And Zion crowns Thy head.
Great thunderbolts of wrath
    Defeat the noise of war;
And true peace reigns when selfish gains
    Entice our greed no more.

Our LORD is to be feared
    By those who would deny
God's matchless splendor and discharge
    The law with but a sigh.
God shall dismiss the proud
    To fret in jealous pride,
And while they yearn, the meek shall learn
    The LORD stands at their side.

# Psalm 77

*A Psalm of Comfort*

Unto You, I cried aloud,
   That my prayer should reach Your ear;
None but God can lift the cloud,
   None to my despair brings cheer.
In the midst of darkest night,
Set my fearful doubts to flight.

In distress, I will recall
   How the LORD my life has blessed;
How the heroes of my race
   Fought for truth and righteousness;
Liberty is their reward,
By the strong arm of the LORD.

In the tempest, You are there,
   Calling forth the flood and fire;
Thunder blasts at Your command,
   If its roar meets Your desire.
For a path, the sea did part,
From Your throne into my heart.

# Psalm 78

*A Psalm of God's Guidance*

"Give ear, my people, to my Law,"
    Thus did the LORD command;
"My words, though cast in parable,
    Your hearts can understand.
To tell your children of my might
    Is all that I demand!"

Each passing generation sings
    The wonders of the LORD,
That those who follow in their steps
    May be of one accord
To keep God's Law above all else,
    And hold God yet adored.

How marvelous the LORD preserved
    Our kindred in distress;
The sea a path did yield, and springs
    Did feed the wilderness.
No less are we today the heirs
    Of truth and righteousness.

# Psalm 79

*A Prayer for Deliverance*

O LORD, the godless boast
    Our legacy is theirs;
Your holy temple lies in ruin,
    Our faith despairs.
Our flesh is torn for meat,
    And blood, like water, shed;
Our bodies wither in the dust,
    Our hope is dead.

How long, O God, how long,
    Your fury, like a fire
Shall blaze until but ash remains
    Of vain desire?
Remember not our sins,
    But mercy to us show;
Let Your compassion meet our need,
    And grace bestow.

# Psalm 80

*A Prayer for Deliverance*


O Shepherd, hear and lead Thy flock,
    As lambs, we crave Thy care;
What strength on earth approaches Thine,
    What mercies can compare?
Restore to us a saving faith,
    The radiance of Thy face
To lighten and reveal the gift
    Of Thy redeeming grace.

Our selfish prayers deserve Thy wrath,
    Our pride, a sudden burst;
We have but stones to serve as bread,
    And tears to quell our thirst.
Restore to us a saving faith,
    The radiance of Thy face
To lighten and reveal the gift
    Of Thy redeeming grace.

Thy lineage, like a vine, once spread
    And flourished in the land;
But now the vineyard fails, the fruit
    Lies withered in the sand.
Restore to us a saving faith,
    The radiance of Thy face
To lighten and reveal the gift
    Of Thy redeeming grace.

# Psalm 81

*A Song of God's Goodness*

O sing to God, our strength;
    In Jacob's God, rejoice!
Let trumpets sound, and with a song
    Lift up your voice!
"I am the LORD your God,"
    Our Maker did declare;
"The same who saves from captive bonds
    And dark despair."

May we unto Thy voice
    Be never deaf to heed,
Or mute to sing the praise of God,
    Our LORD indeed!
"For I shall give the best
    The harvest will afford
Unto the faithful and the just,"
    Thus says the LORD!

# Psalm 82

*A Song of God's Judgment*

Within the congregation
    God with the just shall stand;
The pillars of unrighteousness
    Will shake at God's command.
Injustice meets compassion,
    Contempt discovers grace;
And ev'ry source of our delight
    Is banished from this place.

The wicked shall become as blind,
    And struggle on their way;
To them, as darkest, fearful night
    Appears the brightest day.
They fall, but as they stumble,
    The righteous children dance;
They pass in vain; new life we claim
    For our inheritance.

# Psalm 83

*A Prayer for Deliverance*

In silence, LORD, do not remain;
    Nor hold Thy peace apart from me.
Be still no more; I cannot gain
    The strength I lack, except from Thee.
My foes conspire with one accord
    To work their hate against the LORD.

The nations rise against the land
    A birthright given by Thy word;
And legions meet on ev'ry hand;
    Thine heirs are crushed beneath the sword.
Only by faith secured in Thee
    May we possess the victory.

Disperse their arms as worthless dust;
    Cast them, like chaff, before the wind.
Fill them with shame before the just,
    Bare their deceit, Thy judgment send.
To shame their pride; make them recall
    That Thou alone art LORD of all.

# Psalm 84

*A Psalm of Longing*

How lovely is Thy dwelling place,
 O LORD of hosts, to me;
Within the grandeur of Thy courts
 My soul desires to be.

The sparrow finds a safe retreat,
 Secure she takes her rest;
And in Thy shelter, for her young
 The swallow builds her nest.

How blest are they who in Thy house
 Live out their faithful days;
Their hearts with springs of joy are filled,
 Their lips with songs of praise!

To make my home with Thee, O LORD,
 My hopeful heart aspires;
For there one day outshines the years
 Spent for my own desires.

O LORD, Thou art both sun and shield,
 My sure defense shall be;
How great the happiness they find
 Who set their trust in Thee!

          *The Psalter for Christian Worship*

# Psalm 85

*A Prayer for Deliverance*

The LORD has long with favor looked
    Upon the chosen land;
To Jacob's heirs, the wealth of earth
    Is lavished in their hand.
The captive chains of servitude
    Are loosed, the slaves are free;
And through God's grace, the bonds of sin
    Give way to liberty.

Restore to us salvation, LORD,
    Let Thy displeasure cease;
And still the tempest of Thy wrath
    With gentle winds of peace.
My humble heart the still small voice
    Of Thy love yet attends;
The faithful God from death redeems,
    The fearful, God defends.

Thy steadfast love and faithfulness
    Will meet us face to face;
The arm of justice, mercy sways;
    The righteous, truth embrace.
May wisdom dwell in human law,
    And justice, courts display;
Let righteousness precede Thy steps,
    And guide us on our way.

# Psalm 86

*A Prayer for Deliverance*

Incline Thine ear, O LORD, to me,
    For I am poor, and need Thy care;
My God, the anchor of my trust;
    The truest answer to my prayer.

Thou, LORD, hath shown to me Thy grace,
    In ways beyond my mortal sight;
Before Thy face, I lift my soul;
    To sing Thy praise is my delight!

With steadfast love and mercy sure,
    God hears confession and forgives;
Redeemed the soul in which God dwells,
    And blest the heart wherein God lives!

All nations shall proclaim Thee LORD,
    And at Thy name all knees shall bend
To glorify Thy righteousness,
    And sing Thy praises without end.

# Psalm 87

*A Song in Praise of Zion*

The city of our God is built
    Upon the holy hill;
Her gates, through ages unexcelled;
    Her courts, unchallenged still.

How great the wonders of her past;
    What glories lie in store?
For out of Zion shall the LORD
    Come to us evermore.

All ye who sound the harp and pipe,
    Who songs of hope employ,
The day shall come for you to dance,
    When Zion springs with joy!

# Psalm 88

*A Prayer for Healing*

O let my prayer approach Thee,
   Attend my mournful plight;
I call for help in daylight,
   And cry out in the night.
My soul is full of sorrow,
   As one condemned to die;
Once loved, but now forsaken;
   My song now but a sigh.

Thy anger rests upon me,
   Dark shadows hide my ways;
Can broken arms embrace Thee,
   Can death rise up to praise?
Does Thy declared affection
   Extend beyond the grave?
If I forget to ask Thee,
   Wilt Thou forget to save?

But I have not forgotten
   My weakness and Thy might;
In humble faith, I beg Thee
   To put my fears to flight.
Though all on earth forsake me,
   My lover and my friend;
I hold Thee to Thy promise:
   Be with me to the end.

# Psalm 89a

*A Prayer for Deliverance*


We will ever sing Your mercy,
    Tell abroad Your faithfulness;
Who throughout all generations
    Keeps the covenant to bless.
Sun and stars shall praise Your wonders,
    All the earth, such glories share;
None in heav'n can match Your greatness;
    None below with You compare.

By Your hand is justice measured;
    Judgment rests with You alone;
Truth and mercy go before You,
    Righteousness becomes Your throne.
Blest are they who own Your wisdom,
    Those who live within Your grace;
In Your favor, hold us near You;
    Make our hearts Your dwelling place.

God who swore great things to Judah,
    Her defense and strength and stay,
Makes with equal faith the promise
    To abide with us today.
Loving-kindness shall embrace us,
    Truth attend us all our days;
If we give to God all honor,
    We shall live to sing God's praise!

# Psalm 89b

*A Song of God's Promise*

The chosen of the LORD shall own
    God's blessing full and free;
Uplifted by the arms of faith
    For all the world to see.

The steadfast truth and love of God
    Outweighs the crush of hate;
The LORD bestows on faithful hearts
    True joys to celebrate.

The holy court which God ordained
    Brings justice swift and sure;
To those who live beneath the law,
    God's mercies will endure.

God's covenant forever stands
    As truth for all to claim,
And generations yet to come
    Will sing God's holy name.

# Book IV

## Psalm 90

*A Song of God's Eternity*

LORD, Thou hast been our dwelling place
    From past to coming age the same;
The mountains rise to greet Thy face,
    The earth proclaims her Maker's name.

Each generation fades as grass,
    And flesh as dust returns to sod;
A thousand years spent here below
    Are but as yesterday to God.

Teach us to measure all our days,
    That wisdom may our purpose be;
Each moment guide with righteousness,
    And fill with fervent praise to Thee.

Our mornings may Thou fill with love,
    And show Thy grace when day is past;
That all our life may favor find,
    Till we shall be with Thee at last.

# Psalm 91

*A Wisdom Psalm*


Deep in the shelter of the LORD I dwell,
    And in the shadow of God's love abide;
No pestilence or snare will me assail,
    When God Almighty watches at my side.

Beneath God's hov'ring wings I rest secure,
    With calm assurance that my help is near;
God's loving-kindness my protection sure,
    And e'er attends to banish all my fear.

Since I have made the LORD my dwelling place,
    Home of my care and harbor for my praise;
Great hosts of angels, messengers of grace,
    God sends to keep me safe in all my ways.

"For I, the LORD, have bound you safe in love,
    You need not fear, I will your rescue be";
Since Thou, O LORD, from danger me remove,
    My song shall be Thy praise eternally.

# Psalm 92

*A Song of Thanksgiving*

How good to bring our thanks to God!
    To sing the praises of our LORD!
Each rising day, God's steadfast love,
    Like finest oil on us is poured.

Thy faithfulness I sing by night;
    My songs of joy with darkness clad;
Thy music, LORD, is my delight,
    And all Thy works have made me glad.

The righteous in God's courts shall grow
    And flourish while they have their breath;
The God who sees their righteous days
    Will not forsake them after death.

# Psalm 93

*A Hymn of Praise to God*


The LORD is clad in majesty,
    Adorned in glorious array;
The throne which earth's wide bounds ordained
    Still wears the crown of God today.

The pillars of creation stand,
    Unshaken in their ageless flight;
The raging floods their wrath dispel,
    And meekly wane before God's might.

Thy testimonies, LORD, are fast;
    In holiness, Thy house secure;
From age to age shall Thy decrees
    In righteousness and truth endure.

# Psalm 94

*A Prayer for Deliverance*

Arise, O Judge of earth,
    Enthroned above the clouds;
Send vengeance to the wicked lot;
    Humiliate the proud!

They boast, "God does not see
    The truth behind our lies!
The poor, the needy count for naught,
    As chaff before our eyes."

But Thou, who gave us ears,
    Will not refuse to hear;
Who gave us eyes will not be blind,
    Nor slow to shed a tear.

O teach Thy law, O LORD,
    That I may live aright;
Chastise me when I go astray;
    Uphold me by Thy might.

The steadfast love of God
    Is mine till life is past;
To guide my steps across the years,
    And bring me home at last.

# Psalm 95

*A Call to Worship*

Come, let us sing unto the LORD,
    The Rock of our salvation;
May we rejoice in songs of praise
    Before the God of creation,
By whose design the earth was planned;
The seas were filled at Thy command,
    Thou God of ev'ry nation.

Come, let us praise the LORD of lords,
    Who brings us life and pleasure;
A Shepherd who attends the flock
    With care that none can measure.
Give us desire to hear Thy voice;
The will to make Thy way our choice;
    Thy love our fondest treasure.

# Psalm 96

*A Call To Worship*

O sing new songs unto the LORD,
 With shouts God's name adore;
Proclaim salvation day by day,
 God's glory evermore!
Our God to whom all voices rise
 Is worthy of our praise;
Who formed the earth beneath our feet,
 The sun to light our days.

All lesser idols fade away,
 As wisdom intercedes;
The greatest feats our minds conceive
 Are pale beside God's deeds.
O heav'ns, be glad; O earth, rejoice!
 Your deeds and praise accord
To God, and with creation sing
 The glories of the LORD.

# Psalm 97

*A Hymn of Praise to God*

God reigns! Let earth rejoice!
　Let oceans shout God's might!
Borne up by truth and righteousness,
　God's throne is our delight.
God's fire ignites the clouds
　With judgment swift and just;
The evil find their deeds in vain;
　God's foes are brought to dust.

Vict'ry to those who bow
　In awe before God's sword;
Who place their strong reliance in
　The promise of God's Word.
False idols rise to claim
　The weakness of our pride,
But cannot touch the faithful ones,
　For God stands at our side.

All who would seek the right,
　And evil things deplore,
Find pleasure in the courts of God,
　And comfort evermore.
The radiance of God's light
　Beams joy into our days;
Filled with the glory of God's love,
　Our hearts resound with praise.

# Psalm 98

*A Call to Worship*

Sing new songs to God Almighty,
    Marvel at God's majesty!
In the face of foes around us
    God has brought us victory!
Nations all shall see God's promise,
    Love endure and faith prevail;
Evermore will God be gracious
    To the house of Israel.

Joyful songs of praise and honor
    Earth shall sing with one accord;
Horn and trumpet raise a mighty
    Shout of tribute to our LORD!
Seas and floods rejoice with gladness,
    All the earth God's gifts profess;
Endless grace conceived in mercy,
    Justice born in righteousness.

# Psalm 99

*A Hymn of Praise to God*

God reigns, enthroned on high;
    Let all the earth proclaim
With trembling lips the awesome might
    Of God's great name!
A holy LORD, whose rule
    Is marked with equity;
Whose righteousness to us is bound
    All time to be.

Unto the priests of old
    Who called upon God's name,
The Law was spoken from the clouds,
    And wrought in flame!
To God's commands give heed;
    In faith, endure always;
Let Zion's walls forever ring
    With songs of praise!

# Psalm 100

*A Call To Worship*

Let ev'ry voice on earth resound,
    And joyful hearts hold God adored;
In gladness may God's courts abound
    With songs of praise unto the LORD.

Thou art the LORD, by Thy design
    All we in nature claim our place;
Thy flock, we bind our lives to Thine,
    And rest secure beneath Thy grace.

Before the LORD bring thanks and praise,
    Unfathomed mercies wait in store;
God's goodness blesses all our days,
    God's truth endures for evermore!

# Psalm 101

*A Song of Integrity*

Of loyalty and justice, LORD,
    I ever sing to Thee.
If I pursue the blameless way,
    When will Thou come to me?

My house, my heart, become the place
    Integrity resides;
For evil finds no shelter where
    The truth of God abides.

From willful pride and base deceit
    My spirit far remove;
That I may dwell in faith secure,
    And flourish in Thy love.

# Psalm 102

*A Prayer for Mercy*

Hear Thou my prayer, O LORD,
    My earnest cry to Thee;
That in my hour of utmost need,
    Thy presence sets me free.

My tears have been my drink,
    With ashes for my bread;
Thine anger does my life consume,
    And give me up for dead.

But God in glory reigns
    With grace as well as fire;
To judge with pity and to save
    Is God's supreme desire.

Let Zion be a home
    To those who hold her dear,
That people yet unborn may know
    Their LORD is ever near.

The heav'ns some day shall pass,
    And earth return to sod,
But coming years will see no end
    To love which comes from God.

# Psalm 103

*A Psalm of Thanksgiving*

Bless, O bless the LORD, my soul,
    All within me, praise the LORD!
In the fullness of my life,
    Ever is God's name adored!
Who redeems my sinful soul,
Makes my fainting spirit whole.

Merciful, with grace endued,
    God will judge with righteousness;
Slow to anger or to chide,
    Swift to pardon and to bless.
Though our sin deserves the rod,
More than sparing is our God.

High as heav'n above the earth
    Is the LORD's redeeming love;
Far as east from west is laid,
    So does God our sin remove.
As a parent, pity take;
Cleanse our hearts for Thine own sake.

Like the grass that grows and fades,
    So the cycle of our days;
But God's love is ever sure
    Unto those who sing God's praise.
LORD of heav'n, in faithfulness
May I never cease to bless.

# Psalm 104a

*A Hymn to God: Creator*

O bless the LORD, my soul,
    With might and honor clad;
Who makes the darkest midnight bright,
    The mourning spirit glad.
The heav'ns become God's robe,
    God's brow the stars adorn;
The fire and flame, like messengers,
    On wings of wind are borne.

Earth at God's word was formed,
    And seas the land did drown;
As footstools, hills arose to meet
    The peaks that framed God's crown.
God speaks; the raging flood
    Deserts the fertile plain;
And nevermore its bounds exceeds
    To smother earth again.

Who can recount the good
    Thy hands for us have done;
We day to day rehearse Thy deeds,
    Yet they have just begun.
Let sinners be consumed
    In their own vanity,
Unless they know their sure defeat,
    And claim their grace from Thee.

# Psalm 104b

*A Hymn to God: Sustainer*

O LORD, how marvelous Your works;
    Your wisdom, without peer!
The richest blessings heav'n can boast
    You deign to show us here.

The sea is filled from shore to shore
    With creatures great and small;
The minnows teem the tide with whales;
    God's care extends to all.

They wait for God to give them food,
    Who dwell across the land;
And in the season of God's grace
    They feed from God's own hand.

The absence of the LORD gives rise
    To stubborn, faithless fears;
God's Spirit, feeble life renews;
    God's breath can dry our tears.

Your glory, LORD, always endures,
    Your mercy, all our days;
O may I never cease to fill
    Your courts with songs of praise!

# Psalm 105a

*A Song of Praise to God*


Sing songs of praise and thanks to God,
    Who wondrous deeds has done;
By whose design was life ordained,
    God's strength, the battle won.
The judgments of the LORD are just;
    Earth moves beneath God's voice;
The righteous glory in God's might,
    And faithful hearts rejoice.

Remember well when God's elect
    In bondage bore the chains,
Endured the test of faith and won
    God's favor yet again.
These slaves, redeemed through true belief,
    The tyrant's rod destroyed;
They claimed the blessings of the land
    Which masters once enjoyed.

# Psalm 105b

*A Song of God's Faithfulness*

Rejoice, ye faithful, in the LORD,
    A song of thanks now raise;
For all the goodness to us giv'n,
    Unite to sing God's praise.

The miracles God's grace fulfills
    Are wrought for our avail;
How blest are they whose hearts confirm
    God's love will never fail!

The just rewards of unbelief
    Are fashioned through our fears;
And nightmares, once imagined, gain
    Their flesh when doubt appears.

But to the stalwart in their faith
    God's blessings are displayed;
They sing with joy, the chosen ones
    Whose hope in God is stayed.

# Psalm 106

*A Psalm of Praise*

Our gracious LORD be always praised,
    Give thanks to God above;
The blessings we enjoy on earth
    Are gifts of God's great love.

Remember, LORD, our faithfulness,
    When in Thy courts we meet;
May our degree of righteousness
    Find mercy at Thy feet.

The chosen ones, from bondage freed,
    Were sheltered in Thy fold;
With hands unmoistened by the sea,
    They cast an ox of gold.

The righteous remnant of their tribe
    Redemption claimed from Thee;
When my own judgment shall be due,
    Be gracious unto me.

# BOOK V

## Psalm 107

*A Psalm of Thanksgiving*

Give thanks to God,
    Who all goodness has brought us;
God, whose great love
Shall redeem us forever;
From earth's wide corners,
    God's mercy has sought us;
May God's redemption
Depart from us never.

Hear when we call from
    Amid desolation,
Starving for life,
Yet more frightened of living;
When You, O LORD,
    Offer true consolation,
Let us respond
With a song of thanksgiving.

Hear us, the pris'ners
    Of sin and affliction,
Fast bound in shackles
Of doubt and misgiving;
When You, O LORD,
    Offer strength to conviction,
Let us respond
With a song of thanksgiving.

Hear when the earth
    In its rage would destroy us;
Wind and the sea
Steal our passion for living.
When quiet shelter
    and love You provide us,
Let us respond
With a song of thanksgiving.

*The Psalter for Christian Worship*

# Psalm 108

*A Psalm of Confidence in God*

My heart, O God, is now attuned
   To offer songs of praise!
Awake, my soul, the dawn resounds
   With joy throughout my days!

O may my tongue be never still
   To speak my grateful part
To Thee, who reigns above the clouds,
   Yet dwells within my heart.

Exalt Thyself above the sky,
   And set my eyes on Thee,
That where the faithful find their rest,
   I, too, secure may be.

The lands of earth to Thee belong,
   The desert and the plain;
Reclaim them for Thy kingdom now,
   And bring me home again.

# Psalm 109

*A Prayer for Deliverance*

Be not silent, God of judgment,
    When my foes against me rail;
For I know their hate will perish,
    And Thy righteousness prevail.
In return for love, they curse me;
    At my constant faith, deride;
I can bear their accusations,
    If Thou, LORD, stand at my side.

Help me, LORD, in my affliction;
    Show Thy steadfast love to me;
When Thou bringeth me salvation,
    Vengeance, too, I'll leave to Thee.
With my mouth, I'll sing Thy praises;
    With my heart, Thy love confess;
Crown my life with Thine affection;
    Let me live Thy name to bless.

# Psalm 110

*A Psalm of Deliverance*

Thus spoke the LORD, "I will defend
    The righteous, who at my right hand
Subdue their foes beneath their feet,
    And all their wicked threats withstand."

God shall send forth from Zion's hill
    A mighty scepter to their throne,
That they who rule in righteousness
    Shall never face their foes alone.

How great the pow'r of God to bless;
    Heav'n's richest gifts on us to pour;
God's wrath may shatter disbelief,
    But faith is ours for evermore.

# Psalm 111

*A Hymn of Praise to God*

With my heart, I praise my Maker
    Ever in God's temple sing;
Great and glorious are God's mercies,
    Endless honor shall we bring
To the LORD; let all creation
    With great adoration ring!

God, all gracious and all caring,
    Send Your blessings from above;
If in wrath, Your arm works vengeance,
    Can Your heart with pity move?
May our sins by grace inherit
    Justice tempered with Your love.

All Your laws are sure established,
    Wrought of love and equity;
And the promise of Your mercy
    Shall endure all time to be.
Those whose lips sing of Your glory
    Evermore Your face shall see.

# Psalm 112

*A Wisdom Psalm*

How happy are they, whose eager delight
    Is none but to praise and serve Thee aright;
Who make, LORD, Thy will their unquestioned decree,
    And nurture their children in reverence to Thee.

Forever the LORD will honor the race
    Which worships in awe, and prospers in grace;
In darkness, the godly a radiance shall find,
    And equal compassion for those who are kind.

In presence of foes, the just shall not fear,
    For peace is God's vow, and ever is near;
To those who in confidence rest on God's will,
    God's unmeasured mercies their vict'ry fulfill.

From bountiful stores, God's generous hand
    Shall scatter its good far over the land;
The poor shall inherit the wealth of the proud,
    And tongues of the righteous sing praises aloud!

# Psalm 113

*A Hymn of Praise to God*


Bless the LORD, O saints and servants,
   Praise the might of God's great name;
Ageless, matchless, filled with wonder,
   Yesterday, today, the same.
When the dawn receives the sunrise
   Till the night returns its rays,
Shall the glory of God's goodness
   Be the theme of all our praise.

Who in heav'n can be God's equal,
   Who on earth with God compare?
Who can raise the poor from ashes,
   Lift the needy from despair?
God alone invites the helpless
   With the strong to share reward;
Fields once barren yield a harvest,
   Tongues once silent praise their LORD.

# Psalm 114

*A Hymn of Praise to God*

When the bonds of Thine elect
    Shattered were by Thine own hand;
Judah's house became Thy throne,
    Israel, Thy chosen land.

At their feet, the sea withdrew;
    Through the tides they safely passed;
Hills and mountains skipped as lambs,
    Long in exile, home at last.

Why do earth's dominions shake,
    Floods subside, and shackles fall?
Why, indeed? Like us, they know
    Jacob's God is LORD of all.

# Psalm 115

*A Psalm of Praise to God*

Not unto us, O LORD,
    But let all glory be
A tribute for Thy mercy's sake,
    And truth eternally.

The faithless will inquire,
    "Where may your God be found?"
They blindly seek a god of gold;
    We see Thee all around.

Their idols, like their faith,
    Hold emptiness and pride;
And in their quest for greater gods,
    These soon are cast aside.

But Israel's faith is stayed,
    In Aaron's God secure;
An everlasting help and shield
    Is God, our refuge sure.

The LORD who lights the stars,
    And spins the earth in space
Shall bless us with untold delights,
    And nurture us with grace.

# Psalm 116

*A Psalm of Thanksgiving*

I love the LORD, who heard my voice,
    And answered my most earnest plea;
When snares of death my life would take,
    E'en then, O God, I call on Thee.

O what can I to good return
    For all the bounty from Thy store?
Seen with Thy grace, my highest prize
    Is naught, what can I give Thee more?

I lift salvation's cup from which
    Thou had me drink to seal my vow;
And in the sight of all around,
    I honor my commitment now.

The recompense for what is mine
    Is to exalt Thy name always;
My heart with thanks should ne'er run dry,
    Nor tongue refuse to sing Thy praise.

# Psalm 117

*A Psalm of Praise*

Rejoice in God, you nations all,
    Let tongues God's might record;
For great beyond our fondest dreams
    Are blessings of the LORD.

God's steadfast love is unsurpassed
    By our imagined worth;
God's faithfulness shall far outlive
    The timeless bounds of earth.

# Psalm 118

*A Psalm of Thanksgiving*

Give thanks unto our gracious God,
    Whose love endures forever;
The LORD, our strength and song shall be,
    From whom no fault can sever.
Sing mighty songs of victory,
Both now and for eternity,
    For God will leave us never.

I shall not die, but I shall live,
    And sing God's grace with elation.
Though I deserve no more than death,
    God blesses me with salvation.
The gate that should unyielding be
Is open wide to welcome me,
    Give thanks and adoration!

Upon the stones the builders judged
    Imperfect, weak and tender,
Now rest the corners of God's house,
    Still unsurpassed in splendor.
This is the day the LORD has made;
God is my sun, and God my shade;
    Rejoice, and praise gladly render!

# Psalm 119a

*Meditation on God's Law*

How blest are they whose path is pure,
    Who keep Your Law aright;
And happy they who by true faith
    Find favor in Your sight.

Thou, LORD, commands that holy Law
    Should be our constant guide;
And those who bow to God's decree
    Shall not be cast aside.

O may we ever steadfast be
    In living out Your will;
Whose Law, our counsel will remain;
    Whose love, our comfort still.

# Psalm 119b

*A Prayer for Guidance*

Teach me, O LORD, Your holy Law;
    The will to follow so impart
That I with understanding may
    Observe it with a faithful heart.

Let Your right path be ever mine,
    For in Your precepts I delight;
May selfish gain and empty pride
    Be turned away and put to flight.

Grant us the passion to embrace
    Your constant will amid all strife;
For faith unfalt'ring, grant us grace;
    For righteousness, eternal life.

# Psalm 119c

*A Psalm of Praise*

O Lord, how I adore Your Law,
    The greatest treasure for the least!
It is to me a banquet spread
    Where my most hungry thoughts may feast.

Who in Your Word shall meditate
    Finds truth in heart, and hope in tears;
The wisdom which Your Law imparts
    Outlasts the number of our years.

Withhold my feet from evil snares,
    And keep them on the path less trod;
For sweet Your words unto my mouth,
    And true the precepts of my God!

# Psalm 119d

*A Psalm of Trust*

Thy Word, O LORD, a lamp shall be
    To guide my feet, to light my way;
The darkest path unto my prize
    By Thy rich grace is bright as day.

Revive, O God, this fainting soul;
    Be Thou my stay amid distress;
Teach me Thy law, that I may live
    A life renewed in righteousness.

My heritage, Thy lasting word,
    Which through the years, is ever sure;
May I reflect Thy constant love,
    And know Thy truth shall long endure.

# Psalm 119e

*Thanksgiving for God's Justice*

LORD, Thou art righteous always;
　　Thy judgments, all are wise.
And faithful is the witness
　　Which stands before our eyes.
My fervent zeal consumes me,
　　O let me never cease
To hold Thee in remembrance,
　　And in Thy Word find peace.

Thy Word, so pure and holy,
　　Is more than life to me;
Though strength may fade within me,
　　How great my love for Thee!
From age to age, Thy justice
　　Our saving health assures;
And righteousness, with mercy,
　　From age to age endures.

# Psalm 120

*A Prayer for Deliverance*

In my distress, I cried to God,
    "From vain deceit, LORD, rescue me;
Let not the threats sharp tongues may speak
    Defy the faith I hold in Thee.

Too long has war encompassed me,
    Contention raging without cease;
Help me, amid the conflict, be
    A constant symbol of Thy peace."

# Psalm 121

*A Psalm of Blessing*

I lift my eyes unto the hills,
    From where shall come my help at last?
Whate'er the need, God will provide,
    The LORD, by whom the world was cast.

Each day God is a strength and shield
    Against the onslaught of my foes;
And to the dangers of the night,
    The eyes of God are never closed.

The promise of the LORD is sure:
    To hold me in unyielding care;
Throughout my life, may faith confirm
    That where I am, the LORD is there.

# Psalm 122

*A Psalm of Rejoicing*

How glad was my rejoicing,
    How great my soul's delight,
When into God's own temple
    My friends did me invite!
Long have my feet been planted
    Within the city gates;
And soon I'll claim the promise
    For which my spirit waits.

Jerusalem, the city,
    Where tribes are joined as one,
Where God's elect find justice,
    Where righteousness is done;
And I, a child of David
    And heir to God's decree,
Shall take the place in glory
    That God prepares for me.

Jerusalem, God's city,
    May peace dwell in your walls;
And those who love you prosper,
    Whatever else befalls;
Within your vaulted towers,
    Secure I take my rest;
At peace with God's assurance,
    And with God's favor blessed.

# Psalm 123

*A Prayer for Deliverance*

I lift my eyes to You, O LORD,
    Your throne, earth's canopy;
As masters hold their servants dear,
    So, LORD, remember me.

More like a child than bonded slave,
    I claim Your grace outright;
The proud shall fall, but yet the meek
    Find favor in Your sight.

Your boundless mercies, LORD, outweigh
    The scorn we must endure;
While foes shall fade in their contempt,
    Your love will long endure.

# Psalm 124

*A Psalm of Thanksgiving*

If God had not been on our side,
　　When wars around us rose;
Who would have been the sure defense
　　Against our mortal foes?

Their anger at our presence raged;
　　Their wrath, a swelling tide,
To draw us underneath the flood,
　　Were God not at our side.

The Lord be praised, at whose right hand
　　Our enemies are stayed;
Our lasting shield, the name of God,
　　Who heaven and earth has made.

# Psalm 125

*A Prayer for Deliverance*

Those who place on God reliance
    In despair shall not be moved;
As the mountains hug the valley,
    So embraced are God's beloved.
Everlasting is Mount Zion,
    From creation's dawn till night;
And eternal is God's promise
    Unto those who live aright.

All good blessings shall be given
    To the servants of God's will;
Just rewards and retributions,
    Once conferred, are with us still.
Those who work against God's healing
    Have their ill with ill repaid;
But the faithful of the kingdom
    Find their full redemption made.

# Psalm 126

*A Prayer for Deliverance*

When the LORD brought home our treasure,
    All delights were like a dream;
In defeat, a shout of vict'ry;
    In the sand, a flowing stream.
Mouths that once were parched with anguish
    Now with shouts of joy are filled;
Laughter now displaces sadness
    For the goodness God has willed.

Bring us back to former glory,
    Lost through years of exile's pain;
Generations long forgotten
    Seek God's favor to regain.
Those who plant their seeds with grieving,
    Wetting soil with falling tears,
Shall rejoice in time of harvest,
    Reaping hope for all their years.

# Psalm 127

*A Wisdom Psalm*


Except the house is built by God,
    Its stones for naught are laid;
The city, without God's defense,
    Is feeble and afraid.
To eat the bread of anxious toil
    Makes all our labor vain;
God feeds our cherished souls with rest
    To face our work again.

In every age, the greatest gifts
    God's fullness can accord
Are generations born to claim
    The blessings of the LORD.
The ancient die, the young grow old;
    They, too, shall fade away;
Creation, as God's heritage,
    Begins with each new day.

# Psalm 128

*A Wisdom Psalm*

Blest are they whose adoration
    Of the Lord with awe is filled;
All the good wrought by their labor
    Is their gain, so God has willed.
Righteous minds, infused with justice;
    Steadfast hearts, with love instilled.

Like a fruitful vine they flourish
    Branches of a faithful tree,
So shall children's children gather
    At Thy table praising Thee.
Prayers replete with peace and blessing,
    Rise for all eternity.

# Psalm 129

*A Prayer for Deliverance*

How fervently my foes
  Have fought me from my youth,
Yet their deceit cannot defeat
  God's all-sustaining truth.

They plow their furrows deep,
  And turn my flesh for sod;
Despite their rush, they will not crush
  My constant faith in God.

Let them receive their due,
  According to God's word;
And in their place, confirm through grace,
  The blessings of the LORD.

# Psalm 130

*A Prayer for Deliverance*

From the depths I cry to Thee,
    Savior, LORD, my prayer receive;
Who can stand the press of sin?
    Those who in Thy grace believe.
Mark not my iniquity,
    Lest the burden break my heart;
Not my heart alone, but Thine,
    For with mercy great Thou art.

For the LORD my soul awaits;
    In God's word, my hope is laid;
As the sentries by the dawn
    For their patience are repaid.
Hope in God, O Israel;
    God, whose steadfast love is sure;
Who for us redemption brings;
    God, whose mercies shall endure.

# Psalm 131

*A Psalm of Trust*

O Lord, my heart is not too high,
    Nor do my eyes look far above
The things which You for me appoint,
    Except to hope for Your great love.

A child again in mother's arms,
    My soul at peace in Your accord;
I fix my confidence and hope
    In tender mercies of the Lord.

# Psalm 132

*A Psalm of Praise*

Call to mind, O LORD, the pain;
    Hardships David did endure;
That Your dwelling place should be
    In his heart forever sure.

Come, O God, and dwell in me;
    Clothe my soul in righteousness;
May Your presence know my joy,
    May my pleasure be to bless.

You have promised worthy heirs
    Will inherit Zion's throne;
Who with truth and justice rule,
    And confess You, LORD alone.

You, O LORD, all good extend;
    To my needs Your care provide;
So be in my life that I
    After death with You abide.

# Psalm 133

*A Wisdom Psalm*

How good when all the earth is one,
  And hearts embrace community;
When strife will cease to separate,
  And love binds all in unity.

As oil anointed Aaron's head,
  And dew adorns the mountainside,
So peace and blessing of the LORD
  Within the faithful heart abide.

# Psalm 134

*A Psalm of Blessing*

Come, bless the LORD, ye servants all,
　　Who in God's house by night
Bring to the LORD the highest praise,
　　And to the darkness, light.

Lift up your hands unto the LORD,
　　In confidence secure,
Though earth and heaven pass away,
　　God's goodness shall endure.

# Psalm 135

*A Hymn of Praise*

O praise God's name together,
    You servants of the LORD;
O LORD, for all Your favor
    To us, You are adored!
Within Your holy temple,
    Before Your sacred throne,
The chosen heirs of Jacob
    Proclaim You God alone!

O LORD, no mind can measure
    The greatness of Your might;
You gave the earth its orbit,
    And set the stars to flight.
The clouds You raised in heaven
    Give to the fields their rain;
Your Word lifts waves from oceans,
    And mountains from the plain.

False gods may rise before us,
    Their vanity display;
But as the hands that made them,
    They, too, shall fade away.
Your Name, O God Almighty,
    Endures for endless days;
And newborn generations
    Unite to sing Your praise.

# Psalm 136

*A Psalm of Thanksgiving*

O give thanks unto the LORD,
    Who above all gods shall reign;
Sing your praise with one accord,
    Ever in God's fold remain.
For God's steadfast love is sure,
    And forever shall endure!

Praise the wonder of God's might,
    Who the earth and seas displayed;
God, who brought to darkness light,
    In whose image, we are made.
For God's steadfast love is sure,
    And forever shall endure!

More than our imagined grace
    Are the mercies of our God;
Hope is ours, if we but place
    Our reliance in God's Word.
For God's steadfast love is sure,
    And forever shall endure!

# Psalm 137

*A Lament*

By the streams of Babylon
    Wept the nation Israel;
Harps hung mute on willow boughs;
    Tears from captive eyelids fell.
"Sing us one of Zion's songs!"
    Our tormentors mocked our grief;
How can we as strangers here
    Bow before their unbelief?

If Jerusalem should fade
    From my fondest thoughts, I pray,
Let my strength alike disperse,
    And my tongue become as clay.
To abide within Thy walls
    Is the greatest joy to me;
Vanquish those who scorn Thy throne;
    Bring me home to dwell with Thee.

# Psalm 138

*A Psalm of Thanksgiving*

O LORD, my heart will sing,
    I give Thee thanks and praise,
And in Thy holy temple bow
    Throughout my days.
Thy steadfast love in faithfulness,
    O God, let shower from above.

God answered when I called,
    Responding to my need;
The rulers of the earth shall name
    Thee LORD indeed!
The proud will fall, their boasts are vain,
    The meek of earth shall o'er them reign.

Though dangers gather round,
    O, LORD, preserve my life;
And by Thy strong and forceful arm
    I conquer strife.
God will give heed, my hopes fulfill,
    And keep the vow to love me still.

# Psalm 139

*A Prayer for Deliverance*

Thou, O LORD, hast searched and known me,
　　When I rest, and when I rise;
Not a single thought I cherish
　　Is kept secret from Thine eyes.
Ev'ry word my lips would murmur
　　Needs no speech to make it known;
All I do, ere it be started,
　　Is as done to Thee alone.

Whither shall I flee Thy Spirit?
　　From Thy presence, vanish where?
Heights of heaven, darkest shadows
　　Hide me not, for Thou art there.
If I take the wings of morning,
　　And in earth's far corner stand;
Even there Thy love will find me,
　　Hold me fast within Thy hand.

In the brilliance of Thy glory,
　　Darkest night is bright as day;
Shadows flee the path before me,
　　When Thy wisdom lights my way.
Thou who knit my parts together,
　　Knew my life before my birth,
Sees my faults, yet trusts my promise
　　Far beyond my feeble worth.

LORD, how precious is Thy favor
　　Shown in Thy goodwill to me;
To the godless in their rancor,
　　Let me Thy confessor be.
Search, O LORD, my heart's ambitions,
　　Thoughts my mouth would dare not say;
Judge with mercy, and preserve me
　　In the everlasting way.

# Psalm 140

*A Prayer for Deliverance*

From destructive threats, O Lord,
    From the evil all around,
Let Your strength my soul preserve,
    Refuge in Your arms be found.

Like a serpent, would they strike,
    Sharp against Your servant's heel;
Fierce are they who force my fate,
    Fortune, life, and faith would steal.

Yet I know, You are my God,
    Who has seen me through distress;
My salvation, You will send
    Vict'ry for my righteousness.

Ever shall the Lord supply
    Goodness as our needs demand;
Through God's justice, by God's grace,
    May we in God's presence stand.

# Psalm 141

*A Prayer for Deliverance*

I cry to Thee;
Make haste to hear me,
    LORD, on Thee I call;
In my distress,
    Thou art my all in all.
My prayer ascends as
    Incense to the sky;
    My hope is nigh.

May I be pure;
Guard me from evil;
    Let my lips proclaim
My sure salvation
    In Thy holy name.
So guide my footsteps
    On Thy sheltered ways
    Through all my days.

*The Psalter for Christian Worship*

# Psalm 142

*A Prayer for Deliverance*

Unto my God I cried aloud,
   My supplication poured;
In my distress, God heard my prayer;
   My fainting soul restored.
The deepest valleys of my life
   Are plains before the LORD.

Around me camp the hosts of death,
   Who would my path assail;
None but the LORD stand at my side,
   And none but God prevail.
Therefore, my LORD, I trust in Thee,
   Whose promise will not fail.

O save me from their raging hate,
   Which would my faith destroy;
Before the wiles of their deceit,
   Thy saving grace employ,
That I may find my heart's delight,
   And revel in Thy joy!

# Psalm 143

*A Prayer for Deliverance*

To my prayer, LORD, bend Thine ear;
    Faithful in Thy vow to hear me.
Let Thy righteousness pronounce
    Such a judgment as would cheer me.
None is worthy of Thy favor,
But by grace Thy mercy savor.

Thou who in the ancient past
    Wrought great deeds for our salvation;
Take our outstretched hands in Thine,
    Lift us from our desolation.
Help me, for my spirit fails;
Only Thy rich love prevails.

As the morning claims the dawn,
    Light appears to quell night's blindness;
In the radiance of Thy face,
    Bathe me with Thy loving-kindness.
Fill me with the sacred leaven
That will raise my soul to heaven.

*The Psalter for Christian Worship*

# Psalm 144

*A Lament*

Blest be God, who is my fortress,
    By whose hand my own is led;
Those who would my life endanger
    Shall themselves be lost instead.
What am I that God should prosper
    Me with righteousness always?
Turn the boasts of my ambitions
    Into heartfelt songs of praise.

Stretch Thy hand, O my Redeemer,
    Rescue me from hostile plight;
With Thy sword, a blazing pattern
    Slash across my darkest night.
Then will I new songs of vict'ry
    Sing to Thee, who at my side
Brought my foes to their destruction,
    Swept them up in their own pride.

Happy those who claim Thy mercy,
    Blest are they who know Thy love;
Sons and daughters, strong and vibrant,
    In Thy wisdom live and move.
May our lives be such to merit
    Some degree of all Thy store;
In Thy house, may we find favor
    And abide for evermore.

# Psalm 145

*A Psalm of Praise*

I will ever sing Thy praises,
  For all time, Thy name I'll bless;
Without peer is Thy great glory,  .
  Limitless Thy righteousness.
Each new generation numbers
  All Thy blessings as their own;
To the earth's most far-flung regions
  Is Thy majesty made known.

Thou art gracious, full of mercy,
  Slow to anger, quick to love;
Saints below may glimpse Thy kingdom
  In the lofty skies above.
In this life, the best we savor
  Is but common fare to Thee;
All the riches earth can harvest
  Cannot match Thy majesty.

For the LORD is ever faithful
  To supply our deepest need;
Justice grows from every judgment,
  Wholesome bread from every seed.
God is ne'er too far to hear us,
  Never deaf to our demands;
Those who love and trust the promise
  Rest secure within God's hand.

# Psalm 146

*A Psalm of Praise*

Bless the LORD, give praise and honor
    Unto God who lends me breath;
May my tongue God's greatness never
    Cease to tell before my death.
And in songs of sovereign goodness,
    Let me sing beyond the grave;
God, whose grace my life to ransom,
    God, whose will my soul to save.

Blest are they whose hope is vested
    In the God of Israel;
In the hour of deepest anguish,
    God's provisions will not fail;
Freedom for the shackled spirit,
    Strength and stay to those who fall;
Blessings offered without measure,
    Righteousness enough for all.

# Psalm 147a

*A Psalm of Praise*

Praise to the LORD, for it is good to praise;
God, who the loving heart with love repays;
Whose gracious kindness blesses us always,
    Alleluia!

God makes the broken heart rejoice once more;
A healing ointment on our wounds will pour;
Our feeble spirits shall the LORD restore,
    Alleluia!

Great is the LORD, abundant in the care
Provided for all creatures everywhere;
To God's rich love, no earthly loves compare,
    Alleluia!

Our greatest strength is weakness in God's sight;
In our ambitions, God does not delight,
But for our constant will to live aright,
    Alleluia!

# Psalm 147b

*A Psalm of Praise*


Sing, Jerusalem, God's favor;
    Shout, O Zion, God's goodwill;
Who, in time of tribulation,
    Shall be our Defender still.
Alleluia, alleluia!
    Let your praise God's temple fill!

God brings peace within our borders;
    Fills our barns with finest grain;
Snow, like fleece, the fields may cover,
    But with spring, new life they gain.
Alleluia, alleluia!
    Faithful shall our LORD remain.

For all times God's Word is with us;
    Ever swift the LORD's decree;
Steadfast always to the nations
    Who to God shall faithful be.
Alleluia, alleluia!
    Constant is our praise to Thee.

# Psalm 148

*A Psalm of Praise*


Praise God in the highest heaven,
    Sun and moon and stars in space;
Sing, ye angels, of God's goodness;
    Tell, ye ordered skies, God's grace.
Alleluia, alleluia!
    Who but God your course can trace?

All the earth will shout God's praises,
    Mountain peaks and ocean floor;
Wind and fire and beast and forest,
    Hill and desert, vale and shore.
Alleluia, alleluia!
    Honor God whom you adore.

Rise, O child of God, in wonder
    At creation's majesty;
Young and old, God's glory claiming,
    Praise the LORD in unity.
Alleluia, alleluia!
    Now and for eternity.

# Psalm 149

*A Psalm of Praise*

Praise the LORD, new songs employ, Alleluia!
Sing to God, who is your joy, Alleluia!
Israel, with one accord, Alleluia!
Lift your voice unto the LORD, Alleluia!

Let your feet be still no more, Alleluia!
Dance, your Maker to adore, Alleluia!
Strike the timbrel and the lyre, Alleluia!
Your delight is God's desire, Alleluia!

Heirs to grace, now celebrate, Alleluia!
God in righteousness is great, Alleluia!
Justice shall outlast our days, Alleluia!
If we lose ourselves in praise, Alleluia!

# Psalm 150

*A Doxology*

Let ev'ry heart lift up God's name in praise;
Each voice a song within this temple raise
To God, whose goodness follows all our days:
   Alleluia, alleluia!

The trumpet sounds the power of God's might;
The pipe and strings put all despair to flight;
And spirits dance with cymbals clear and bright:
   Alleluia, alleluia!

Praise ye the LORD in anthems strong and sure,
With bold assurance, confidence secure,
Though breath shall cease, God's love will long endure:
   Alleluia, alleluia!

# Index of
# Suggested Tunes

| Psalm | Meter | Tunes |
|---|---|---|
| 1 | LM | CANONBURY *or* ROCKINGHAM |
| 2 | 8.7.8.7 D | EBENEZER |
| 3 | LM | WHEN JESUS WEPT |
| 4 | 10.10.9.10 | SLANE |
| 5 | LM | ROCKINGHAM |
| 6 | 7.7.7.7.7.7 | LUX PRIMA *or* DIX |
| 7 | CM | MORNING SONG *or* ST. AGNES |
| 8 | 8.6.8.8.6 | REST |
| 9 | 6.7.6.7.6.6.6.6 | NUN DANKET ALLE GOTT |
| 10 | 7.7.7.7 D | ABERYSTWYTH |
| 11 | CMD | RESIGNATION |
| 12 | CM | LAND OF REST |
| 13 | 7.6.7.6 D | LLANGLOFFAN |
| 14 | CM | DUNDEE |
| 15 | LM | GERMANY *or* WINCHESTER NEW |
| 16 | LM | TALLIS' CANON *or* CONDITOR ALME SIDERUM |
| 17 | 8.7.8.7 | CHARLESTOWN *or* STUTTGART |
| 18 | CMD | FOREST GREEN |
| 19 | CMD | ELLACOMBE |
| 20 | 7.6.7.6 D | LLANGLOFFAN |
| 21 | CM | ST. ANNE |
| 22a | 7.6.7.6 D | PASSION CHORALE |
| 22b | CMD | NOEL |
| 23 | CMD | FOREST GREEN |
| 24 | 10.10.10.10 | TOULON |
| 25 | CM | MORNING SONG *or* MARTYRDOM |
| 26 | LM | ROCKINGHAM *or* GERMANY |
| 27 | 8.7.8.7 D | ABBOT'S LEIGH *or* BEACH SPRING |
| 28 | LM | DU MEINER SEELEN |

| | | |
|---|---|---|
| 29 | 8.7.8.7 D | AUSTRIAN HYMN *or* HYFRYDOL |
| 30 | 8.7.8.7 D | ABBOT'S LEIGH *or* HYFRYDOL |
| 31a | LM | WAREHAM |
| 31b | 9.8.9.8 | ST. CLEMENT |
| 32 | 7.6.7.6 D | MUNICH |
| 33 | CMD | ELLACOMBE |
| 34 | CM | ST. MAGNUS *or* ST. STEPHEN |
| 35 | LM | DEO GRACIAS *or* HEBRON |
| 36 | LM | O WALY WALY |
| 37 | 7.6.7.6 D | NYLAND |
| 38 | LM | ERHALT UNS, HERR *or* KEDRON |
| 39 | CM | LAND OF REST |
| 40 | 7.6.8.6.8.6.8.6 | ST. CHRISTOPHER |
| 41 | LM | GERMANY *or* TRURO |
| 42 | 9.8.9.8 | ST. CLEMENT |
| 43 | CMD | KINGSFOLD |
| 44 | CMD | KINGSFOLD *or* NOEL |
| 45a | 7.7.7.7 | MONKLAND |
| 45b | 7.7.7.7.7.7 | RATISBON |
| 46 | 8.7.8.7.8.7 | WESTMINSTER ABBEY |
| 47 | 8.7.8.7.8.7.7 | CWM RHONDDA |
| 48 | 10.10.11.11 | LYONS *or* HANOVER |
| 49 | 7.6.7.6 D | AURELIA *or* EWING |
| 50 | CMD | ELLACOMBE *or* AMESBURY |
| 51 | CM | ST. FLAVIAN *or* DUNDEE |
| 52 | 8.7.8.7 D | EBENEZER |
| 53 | 7.7.7.7 D | ABERYSTWYTH |
| 54 | CM | MARTYRDOM *or* LAND OF REST |
| 55 | LM | ERHALT UNS, HERR *or* ROCKINGHAM |
| 56 | CM | ST. STEPHEN *or* CRIMOND |
| 57 | 7.6.7.6 D | LLANGLOFFAN |
| 58 | 8.7.8.7 D | EBENEZER |
| 59 | LM | WHEN JESUS WEPT *or* ROCKINGHAM |
| 60 | LM | KEDRON *or* BOURBON |

| | | |
|---|---|---|
| 61 | 8.7.8.7 | STUTTGART |
| 62 | LM | WAREHAM *or* ROCKINGHAM |
| 63 | CM | CAITHNESS *or* ST. AGNES |
| 64 | CM | ST. STEPHEN *or* MORNING SONG |
| 65 | 11.11.11.11 | ST. DENIO |
| 66a | 7.7.7.7.7.7 | RATISBON |
| 66b | CM | ST. PETER *or* MCKEE |
| 67 | 8.7.8.7 D | HYFRYDOL |
| 68 | 6.6.11.6.6.11 D | ASH GROVE |
| 69 | 9.8.9.8.8.8 | WER NUR DEN LIEBEN GOTT |
| 70 | 8.7.8.7 | STUTTGART |
| 71 | CM | AZMON |
| 72 | 8.7.8.7.6.6.6.6.7 | EIN' FESTE BURG |
| 73 | SMD | TERRA BEATA |
| 74 | 7.7.7.7 D | ABERYSTWYTH |
| 75 | 6.7.6.7.6.6.6.6 | NUN DANKET ALLE GOTT |
| 76 | SMD | TERRA BEATA |
| 77 | 7.7.7.7.7.7 | ARFON *or* DIX |
| 78 | 8.6.8.6.8.6 | MORNING SONG |
| 79 | 6.6.8.4 D | LEONI |
| 80 | CMD | KINGSFOLD *or* FOREST GREEN |
| 81 | 6.6.8.4 D | LEONI |
| 82 | 7.6.7.6 D | LLANGLOFFAN |
| 83 | 8.8.8.8.8.8 | DAS NEUGEBORNE KINDELEIN *or* VATER UNSER |
| 84 | CM | LAND OF REST |
| 85 | CMD | FOREST GREEN |
| 86 | LM | WAREHAM *or* ROCKINGHAM |
| 87 | CM | AZMON |
| 88 | 7.6.7.6 D | LLANGLOFFAN |
| 89a | 8.7.8.7 D | ABBOT'S LEIGH |
| 89b | CM | IRISH *or* ST. ANNE |
| 90 | LM | DUKE STREET *or* TRURO |
| 91 | 10.10.10.10 | EVENTIDE |

| 92 | LM | TALLIS' CANON |
|---|---|---|
| 93 | LM | BOURBON or WINCHESTER NEW |
| 94 | SM | FESTAL SONG |
| 95 | 8.7.8.7.8.8.7 | MIT FREUDEN ZART |
| 96 | CMD | ELLACOMBE or ALL SAINTS NEW |
| 97 | SMD | DIADEMATA |
| 98 | 8.7.8.7 D | BEACH SPRING or HOLY MANNA |
| 99 | 6.6.8.4 D | LEONI |
| 100 | LM | OLD HUNDREDTH or DUKE STREET |
| 101 | CM | DUNDEE |
| 102 | SM | ST. BRIDE or ST. MICHAEL |
| 103 | 7.7.7.7.7.7 | RATISBON or LUX PRIMA |
| 104a | SMD | DIADEMATA |
| 104b | CM | ST. PETER |
| 105a | CMD | ELLACOMBE |
| 105b | CM | TALLIS' ORDINAL or ST. FLAVIAN |
| 106 | CM | ST. STEPHEN or ST. ANNE |
| 107 | 11.11.11.11 | O QUANTA QUALIA |
| 108 | CM | MORNING SONG |
| 109 | 8.7.8.7 D | NETTLETON |
| 110 | LM | DUKE STREET |
| 111 | 8.7.8.7.8.7 | WESTMINSTER ABBEY |
| 112 | 10.10.11.11 | LYONS or HANOVER |
| 113 | 8.7.8.7 D | ABBOT'S LEIGH |
| 114 | 7.7.7.7 | AUS DER TIEFE RUFE ICH or<br>NUN KOMM, DER HEIDENHEILAND |
| 115 | SM | ST. MICHAEL or FESTAL SONG |
| 116 | LM | ROCKINGHAM |
| 117 | CM | AZMON |
| 118 | 8.7.8.7.8.8.7 | MIT FREUDEN ZART or NUN FREUT EUCH |
| 119a | CM | WINCHESTER OLD |
| 119b | LM | WAREHAM |
| 119c | LM | WINCHESTER NEW |
| 119d | LM | O WALY WALY |

| 119e | 7.6.7.6 D | AURELIA *or* EWING |
|------|-----------|--------------------|
| 120 | LM | WINCHESTER NEW *or* GERMANY |
| 121 | LM | PUER NOBIS NASCITUR |
| 122 | 7.6.7.6 D | EWING *or* MUNICH |
| 123 | CM | ST. FLAVIAN |
| 124 | CM | ST. ANNE |
| 125 | 8.7.8.7 D | BEACH SPRING *or* HYFRYDOL |
| 126 | 8.7.8.7 D | IN BABILONE |
| 127 | CMD | KINGSFOLD *or* ST. MATTHEW |
| 128 | 8.7.8.7.8.7 | REGENT SQUARE *or* WESTMINSTER ABBEY |
| 129 | SM | ST. THOMAS |
| 130 | 7.7.7.7 D | ABERYSTWYTH |
| 131 | LM | ROCKINGHAM |
| 132 | 7.7.7.7 | AUS DER TIEFE RUFE ICH *or* SONG 13 |
| 133 | LM | GERMANY |
| 134 | CM | LAND OF REST |
| 135 | 7.6.7.6 D | WIE LIEBLICH IST DER MAIEN *or* ELLACOMBE |
| 136 | 7.7.7.7.7.7 | DIX *or* LUX PRIMA |
| 137 | 7.7.7.7 D | ABERYSTWYTH |
| 138 | 6.6.6.6.8.8 | DARWALL'S 148TH |
| 139 | 8.7.8.7 D | HYFRYDOL *or* BLAENHAFREN |
| 140 | 7.7.7.7 | AUS DER TIEFE RUFE ICH *or* SONG 13 |
| 141 | 4.10.10.10.4 | ORA LABORA |
| 142 | 8.6.8.6.8.6 | MORNING SONG |
| 143 | 7.8.7.8.8.8 | LIEBSTER JESU |
| 144 | 8.7.8.7 D | IN BABILONE *or* BEACH SPRING |
| 145 | 8.7.8.7 D | HYFRYDOL |
| 146 | 8.7.8.7 D | ABBOT'S LEIGH *or* BEECHER |
| 147a | 10.10.10.4 | ENGELBERG |
| 147b | 8.7.8.7.8.7 | WESTMINSTER ABBEY |
| 148 | 8.7.8.7.8.7 | LAUDA ANIMA |
| 149 | 7.7.7.7 | LLANFAIR |
| 150 | 10.10.10.4 | SINE NOMINE |

# Index of Liturgical Use

| Sunday or Festival | Year A | Year B | Year C |
|---|---|---|---|
| *Advent* | | | |
| 1st Sunday of Advent | 122 | 80 | 25 |
| 2nd Sunday of Advent | 72 | 85 | — |
| 3rd Sunday of Advent | 146 | 126 | — |
| 4th Sunday of Advent | 80 | 89a | 80 |
| *Christmas* | | | |
| Christmas Eve | 96 | 96 | 96 |
| Nativity of Jesus Christ/ Christmas Day (at dawn) | 97 | 97 | 97 |
| Nativity of Jesus Christ/ Christmas Day | 98 | 98 | 98 |
| 1st Sunday after Christmas Day | 148 | 148 | 148 |
| 2nd Sunday after Christmas Day | 147b | 147b | 147b |
| Epiphany of the Lord or Sunday before Epiphany | 72 | 72 | 72 |
| *Ordinary Time* | | | |
| Baptism of the Lord | 29 | 29 | 29 |
| 2nd Sunday in Ordinary Time | 40 | 139 | 36 |
| 3rd Sunday in Ordinary Time | 27 | 62 | 19 |
| 4th Sunday in Ordinary Time | 15 | 111 | 71 |
| 5th Sunday in Ordinary Time | 112 | 147a | 138 |
| 6th Sunday in Ordinary Time | 119a | 30 | 1 |
| 7th Sunday in Ordinary Time | 119b | 41 | 37 |
| 8th Sunday in Ordinary Time | 131 | 103 | 92 |
| Transfiguration of the Lord | 2, 99 | 50 | 99 |

## Lent

| | | | |
|---|---|---|---|
| Ash Wednesday | 51 | 51 | 51 |
| 1st Sunday in Lent | 32 | 25 | 91 |
| 2nd Sunday in Lent | 121 | 22b | 27 |
| 3rd Sunday in Lent | 95 | 19 | 63 |
| 4th Sunday in Lent | 23 | 107 | 32 |
| 5th Sunday in Lent | 130 | 15, 119 | 126 |

## Holy Week

| | | | |
|---|---|---|---|
| Passion/Palm Sunday (6th Sunday in Lent) | 31b, 118 | 31b, 118 | 31b, 118 |
| Monday of Holy Week | 36 | 36 | 36 |
| Tuesday of Holy Week | 71 | 71 | 71 |
| Wednesday of Holy Week | 70 | 70 | 70 |
| Maundy Thursday | 116 | 116 | 116 |
| Good Friday | 22a | 22a | 22a |

## Easter

| | | | |
|---|---|---|---|
| Easter Vigil | 16, 19, 42, 43, 46, 98, 114, 136, 143 | 16, 19, 42, 43, 46, 98, 114, 136, 143 | 16, 19, 42, 43, 46, 98, 114, 136, 143 |
| Resurrection of the Lord/Easter | 118 | 118 | 118 |
| Easter Evening | 114 | 114 | 114 |
| 2nd Sunday of Easter | 16 | 133 | 118, 150 |
| 3rd Sunday of Easter | 116 | 4 | 30 |
| 4th Sunday of Easter | 23 | 23 | 23 |
| 5th Sunday of Easter | 31a | 22b | 148 |
| 6th Sunday of Easter | 66 | 98 | 67 |
| Ascension of the Lord | 47, 93 | 47, 93 | 47, 93 |

| | | | |
|---|---|---|---|
| 7th Sunday of Easter | 68 | 1 | 97 |
| Day of Pentecost | 104b | 104b | 104b |

<table>
<tr><td colspan="4" align="center">Ordinary Time</td></tr>
</table>

| | | | |
|---|---|---|---|
| Trinity Sunday | 8 | 29 | 8 |
| 9th Sunday in Ordinary Time | 46 | 139 | 96 |
| 10th Sunday in Ordinary Time | 33 | 138 | 146 |
| 11th Sunday in Ordinary Time | 116 | 20 | 5 |
| 12th Sunday in Ordinary Time | 86 | 9, 133 | 42, 43 |
| 13th Sunday in Ordinary Time | 13 | 130 | 77 |
| 14th Sunday in Ordinary Time | 45b | 48 | 30 |
| 15th Sunday in Ordinary Time | 119d | 24 | 82 |
| 16th Sunday in Ordinary Time | 139 | 89b | 52 |
| 17th Sunday in Ordinary Time | 105, 128 | 14 | 85 |
| 18th Sunday in Ordinary Time | 17 | 51 | 107 |
| 19th Sunday in Ordinary Time | 105 | 130 | 50 |
| 20th Sunday in Ordinary Time | 133 | 111 | 80 |
| 21st Sunday in Ordinary Time | 124 | 84 | 71 |
| 22nd Sunday in Ordinary Time | 105 | 45a | 81 |
| 23rd Sunday in Ordinary Time | 149 | 125 | 139 |
| 24th Sunday in Ordinary Time | 114 | 19 | 14 |
| 25th Sunday in Ordinary Time | 105 | 1 | 79 |
| 26th Sunday in Ordinary Time | 78 | 124 | 91 |
| 27th Sunday in Ordinary Time | 19 | 26 | 137 |
| 28th Sunday in Ordinary Time | 106 | 22a | 66a |
| 29th Sunday in Ordinary Time | 99 | 104a | 119c |
| 30th Sunday in Ordinary Time | 90 | 34 | 65 |

| | | | |
|---|---|---|---|
| 31st Sunday in Ordinary Time | 107 | 146 | 119e |
| All Saints' Day | 34 | 24 | 149 |
| 32nd Sunday in Ordinary Time | 78 | 127 | 98, 145 |
| 33rd Sunday in Ordinary Time | 123 | — | — |
| Christ the King (or Reign of Christ) | 100 | 132 | — |

# Notes